Truths & Contradictions:
Life-Changing Experiences in Afghanistan

Pamela Thompson

Truths & Contradictions: Life-Changing Experiences in Afghanistan

Written by Pamela Thompson

Copyright © 2025 by Pamela Thompson

Published by Raspberry Press
www.raspberrypress.ca

All rights reserved. No part of this publication may be used or reproduced in any manner whatsoever without written permission of the author, except in the case of brief quotations embodied in critical articles or reviews.

Paperback ISBN 978-1-0692485-0-3
Ebook ISBN 978-1-0692485-1-0

Praise for Truths & Contradictions

"Through *Truths & Contradictions*, Pamela Thompson takes us on a journey that is equal parts personal growth and cultural exploration. Her reflections on living and working in a war zone challenge us to think differently about courage, adaptability, and the meaning of leadership. A truly inspiring read."

-Lisa Marie Platske, Leadership and Human Behavior Expert, Author of 7 Books, and on Forbes.com

"In *Truth and Contradictions*, Pamela Thompson brings the reader directly into the courageous lives of her Afghan colleagues and friends. Through her compassionate narrative, we are immersed in times of despair and hope covering decades of war and attempts at peace. It is a guide for anyone who cares about the plight of women and social justice. A vital read for those wishing to gain insights into the complex history and current challenges of Afghanistan."

-Jennifer Hatfield, PhD, Professor Emorata, Department of Community Health Sciences Senior Global Health and Gender Equity Advisor, Cumming School of Medicine, University of Calgary

"This is a story of courage – both of Afghan women who have endured decades of turmoil and of Pamela Thompson, who dared to immerse herself in their world. *Truths & Contradictions* is a profound reminder of the strength and resilience of women everywhere, and an inspiring call to action for advocates of equality and empowerment."

-Shahnaz Qayumi, Faculty, Langara College, COO Partnership Afghanistan (Canada)

"Pamela Thompson's *Truths & Contradictions* is a compelling exploration of leadership, especially during times of uncertainty and conflict. Her journey invites us to redefine resilience and leadership through the values of connection, courage, and cross-cultural understanding. This book is an essential read for women leaders looking for inspiration as they navigate their own pivotal moments."

-Roula Eid, Leadership Strategist and Motivational Speaker

"If you are curious about other cultures and religions, you will enjoy *Truths and Contradictions*. Pamela Thompson weaves history of Afghanistan into sharing her personal experience with the Afghan people and culture as a Canadian woman working and living in Kabul among roses and bombs. In 2024 she interviewed Afghan colleagues and friends seeking to clarify, in their own words, truths and contradictions of Afghan culture and Islam religion."

-Bonnie Fatio, Founder, Inspired Women Lead and Author of *A Fire in Her Belly*

"A window into a world that few have experienced firsthand, Pamela weaves story with strategy to provide us with insights for how we can navigate and influence these times as global citizens and co-creators who share one planet, even if our cultures differ."

-Christine Arylo, MBA, Leadership Advisor, Author and Wisdom Teacher

Acknowledgements

To those Afghan women and men who took time out of their busy lives to be interviewed and shared their poignant stories with me.

To the many women and men with whom I worked while in Afghanistan who made my experience positive.

To my loving partner Alan for his unwavering support.

To Cheryl Fountain and her team at Raspberry Press who supported me in birthing this book.

Contents

Author's Notes		xi
Prologue		xiii
Introduction		xv
Chapter 1:	Preparing for Mission #1	15
Chapter 2:	First Impressions	17
Chapter 3:	My First Day at Work	23
Chapter 4:	Life in Our Compound	29
Chapter 5:	Getting Down to Business	39
Chapter 6:	A Memorable Lunch Hour	49
Chapter 7:	Interesting Characters	55
Chapter 8:	Christmas Holidays	59
Chapter 9:	Back in the Saddle	63
Chapter 10:	Last Days of Mission #1	69
Chapter 11:	Heading Home and Re-entry	77
Chapter 12:	Deepening My Understanding	81
Chapter 13:	Mission #2	121
Chapter 14:	Truths and Contradictions	125
Chapter 15:	Personal Reflections	145
Chapter 16:	The Future of Afghanistan: The Way Forward	149
About the Author		159

Truths & Contradictions:

Life-Changing Experiences in Afghanistan

Author's Notes

This is a work of creative nonfiction. The names of the characters within have been changed to protect their anonymity. The context has been modified in some cases. That said, the experiences are real and at times raw.

My "why" in writing this book is to dispel myths about Afghans, Afghanistan and Islam, and to help people understand the resilience, courage and humanitarian focus of many of the Afghan people. My larger mission is to help build peace and understanding in the world because when we are curious and seek to understand, I believe there can be no war or open conflict.

My intention is also to assist readers in understanding the history of Afghanistan and why the country has been attacked by invaders for so many years.

The women and men who I worked with and interviewed are nearly all physicians, many of whom have Master's degrees. Their experiences are obviously different from illiterate or barely literate women and men who live in rural areas of Afghanistan.

I am honored to have had the opportunity to live and work in this culturally rich country. I am so sorry that the Afghan people, particularly the women, have and are currently being subjected to so many restrictions and such harsh treatment.

It is painful to me to see how many of the rights of Afghan women have been eroded since the Taliban retook the country in August of 2021. Many are now calling what the Taliban are doing in Afghanistan Gender Apartheid.

I hope I have achieved what I set out to do and after having read the book that you have a better understanding of Afghanistan, the courage and resilience of its people and the plight of Afghan women and girls.

Based on my work in five continents with diverse cultures, religions and languages I believe that at our core we have more similarities than differences. We want to be respected, valued, loved, to belong and most of us care about family. If we viewed everyone we meet and interact with through that lens, do you think there would be war?

Prologue

I believe life is an adventure to be lived to the fullest and I live according to that mantra.

My name is Minerva. You may have "met" me in my previous book "The Exploits of Minerva: Reflections of a Sixty-Something Woman."

From a very young age I knew "in my bones" that I would travel the world and be of service, but I wasn't exactly sure how. I've been fascinated by and curious about people from various backgrounds and cultures from about age 4 and have had the opportunity to live and work on five continents.

I invite you to join me on a life-changing journey of living and working in Afghanistan, and to learn about the resilient men and women I met and connected with while living there. Their stories illuminate the many challenges they have faced, and how each and every one of them wants to make a positive difference in the world.

Introduction

I was feeling restless. The new business I had started 18 months ago wasn't "filling me up" and we weren't making a big enough impact fast enough. I really missed the international work I had been doing prior to launching this new venture.

Realizing I wanted to get "out of my head" and into my body, I had enrolled in a Body-Centered Coaching program. I was really enjoying the course. It was the last class that was being held via teleconference. The facilitator/trainer asked for a volunteer to demonstrate a body-centered decision-making process. As no one raised their hand, I offered to do the demo with her.

Her instructions were: Find a line on the floor. Think about something you really want. Notice any fears, negative beliefs or emotions that come up for you and imagine each one of them as a rock in a knapsack on your back. Now feel how heavy those rocks are. Release them and let them go. Think about what you want and cross that line however you wish. You may walk across it, jump across it, leap across it saying aloud what you want.

I leapt across the line and yelled "I want to play BIG!" Within two weeks I received an email inviting me to throw my hat into the ring for one of three senior positions in the health sector in Afghanistan. One of them had my name written all over it. After thinking about it briefly and knowing in my heart I wanted to apply, I spoke with my partner about the opportunity. After some discussion and sharing how much I felt called to do this work, he heartily supported me to go and work in a war zone initially on a nine month contract. Within a week I did just that, I threw my hat into the ring. Within two more weeks I was part of the interview process. About two months after me declaring I wanted to play BIG, I was on the ground in Kabul, starting a nine-month contract as a Senior Technical Advisor, Policy and Planning with the Ministry of Public Health (MoPH).

You'll never guess what the line on the floor in my office had been. It was an Afghan prayer mat one of my technical team in Pakistan had gifted me some years before!

Chapter 1

PREPARING FOR MISSION #1

After I signed the contract, I was instructed to take an online UN Security course and examination. Some of the things I learned were, if you are taken hostage and thrown in the trunk of a car, what is the best thing to do? If you are dropped in the middle of nowhere, how do you identify where north, south, west and east are? I was starting to wonder what I had signed up for.

I was told to add to my wardrobe long and loose tops that covered my buttocks and to purchase a number of headscarves as I would be expected to cover my head while at work and out and about.

The next couple of weeks were spent planning what I would take for a nine-month mission and stuffing as much as possible into two bags. Soon departure day came. I gave my partner the biggest embrace at the airport, finding it hard to let go and not knowing exactly when I would next see him.

It takes a number of flights to get from where I live to Kabul. I don't sleep on airplanes so after almost two days of travel I arrived tired, yet excited, in Afghanistan.

Chapter 2

FIRST IMPRESSIONS

As we approached Kabul, I had feelings of anticipation and some trepidation. Peering out the window I saw the mountains that surround the densely populated city as brown, and not the lush green I was used to in Canada. I found out later that much of the brown was due to deforestation that happened when the Russians invaded Afghanistan.

As we were close to touching down, I noted the rusted out Russian helicopters littering the airfield. I recall the US military man sitting next to me saying "Those helicopters, when they take off, just dance." They were huge machines, and it was hard to believe that they would or could dance in the air.

Arriving at Customs and Immigration in Kabul was a bit chaotic. There was a line, and people seemed to stay in the line. It took some time to clear Customs and get my luggage. That was another challenge. There were bags and people everywhere! I managed to collect my luggage and headed out toward the exit.

As we were walking out to meet our respective parties, the same soldier cautioned me that no one would come close to the arrivals area to collect me, as there had been too many bombings and threats on the airport. I would have to walk out a ways to meet my party.

Armed with luggage for my estimated nine-month stay, I pushed open the heavy glass doors (and stepped into this new life and new world), and looked for the Head of Mission, the woman who was meeting me. Far off in the distance I saw a Caucasian woman in a head scarf waving. That must be Anita. Off I went to meet her. When I arrived, she greeted me with a strong handshake and shared how happy she was to see me.

Driving through the streets of Kabul I was consciously aware of the strong military presence. Everywhere I looked there were men in fatigues armed with AK-47s. Some of them looked about 16 at most. It was dusty and garbage was strewn about certain parts of the city.

As we reached our compound, my "home" for the next nine months, I noted the high concrete walls covered with barbed wire, like something out of a MASH scene. As we entered the huge gates, I noticed a small wire cage populated by two Afghan guards with AK-47s. Not a welcoming sight. I was later informed that anyone coming to visit the compound had to have their name on a register and be "cleared" by the men in the cage before they were allowed in our compound. Anyone who entered without their name on the register was fair game to be shot at.

I was jetlagged after not having slept for two nights. No time to rest. I was shown to my room which was quite spacious and included a small bathroom of my own. There was also a small kitchen across the hall. I was then oriented to the compound that included two large houses and a smaller dormitory at the front where I later learned the Afghan guards and drivers stayed. Beautiful roses were blooming in the garden.

Within an hour I was assigned a metal helmet and flak jacket. Fortunately, I was able to keep these under my bed and did not have to wear them routinely or carry them with me to work. Soon after I was introduced to Kenneth, the Head of Security, a fifty-something British fellow who looked after me and my fellow consultants and trained the Afghan guards and drivers who took us to and from work.

Kenneth took me on a tour of the "safe room" where I was instructed to head to and lock the door if our compound was attacked, and if anyone tried to come over the wall. The safe room was stocked with dry food and lots of bottled water as well as first aid supplies. I hoped in my "heart of hearts" that I would never have to run to the safe room.

A bit later I was introduced to Maggie, the Deputy Head of Mission who offered to take me shopping for some new headscarves and long tops.

After unpacking, I headed out with Maggie and the Head of Security to an Afghan women's clothing shop that had been cleared by our security folks, and found out that I could only go to places that had been okayed by the Head of Security. I was also told that I was unable to walk in the streets and asked to sign a waiver to say that I understood this and could be sent back to Canada if I disobeyed the security rules.

In the Afghan shop I had fun trying on different tops and finding head scarves to coordinate with them. Maggie was really helpful. At one point she saw a burka, one of those loose blue garments that cover women from head to toe. They only have small mesh slits that cover the mouth and nose. Maggie tried one on to see what the experience was like. She took it off in about two minutes saying she could hardly breathe and exclaimed how she couldn't believe how women could walk in the streets during warm weather and be able to breathe let alone have much visibility.

That night at dinner I met the other 7 consultants who "lived" in the compound. What an interesting group!

TRUTHS AND CONTRADICTIONS

PAMELA THOMPSON

Chapter 3

MY FIRST DAY AT WORK

My first day at the Ministry was one of excitement and anticipation. I awoke early, still quite jet-lagged, looking forward to meeting my team; those Afghans I would be working with. I dressed in my new orange embroidered Afghan top, black pants and matching head scarf that I had thoughtfully laid out the night before. After a small breakfast, as I wasn't really hungry, I climbed into the bulletproof vehicle (a Toyota Land Cruiser) with my armed Afghan driver in convoy followed by a soft-skin jeep with three Afghans armed with AK-47s. That is how I travelled to work each day.

Everywhere I looked there were armed police in fatigues holding on tightly to their AK-47s. There were no lines on the road and the three lanes of traffic seemed to miraculously navigate through the people and animals on the streets leading to the Ministry.

There was a large pile of garbage at the side of the road which apparently had been swept up during the night, that a herd of goats was quickly consuming. The goat herder was leading them and cautiously protecting them from the traffic that was weaving in and out. I thought how curious, at the time. But later, on reflection, thought what a sustainable and healthy way to get rid of garbage! It was really a win-win situation. The goats were getting fed from local garbage and the streets were being vacuumed clean by the goats. Later, I found out that one of the international AID agencies had spent a fair bit of time and money cleaning out the riverbed that ran through Kabul during the dry season, and within a week it was again filled up with plastic bags and bottles.

When we arrived at the Ministry there was a guard station and huge wall and gate. The driver checked in with the guard at the gate and disengaged his pistol before entering. Soon the large metal gate was lifted, and we drove into a small parking area. I got out and walked into the Ministry. There was a long red carpet that covered the worn floor. The building looked old and many people were milling about. I finally found my way to the office I was to work in.

I met with Mustafa, who I would be working closely with. He showed me to my well-worn wooden desk, between two others against the wall at one side of the office. There were large floor to ceiling windows. Suddenly the windows began to rattle and the loud whir, whir, whir of a military helicopter cut the relative silence. It reminded me of MASH, the television series I'd watched years ago.

Soon after, Farzanah, who had the desk beside me, entered the room. She had a warm open face and greeted me formally. Mustafa introduced her. She was a local consultant in policy and planning. She and I would become close friends over the coming months.

Later I was introduced to my strategic planning team. After a short while I realized that the team knew hardly any English and the Team Lead understood about eighty percent of what I was saying. This was the team whose capacity I was to build over the next nine months! Reflecting on that moment I chuckle, but at the time all sorts of questions were running through my head such as, "I don't have a budget for an interpreter/translator. How am I going to communicate with the team let alone build their capacity?" Fortunately, Dr. Sylvie, a French physician who had been working in Afghanistan for more than a decade and was head of a large EU- funded project, came to my rescue. On a handshake she said that anytime I needed to communicate with my team or needed documents translated, she would lend me Musa, an Afghan physician who spoke good English. She guaranteed me about 15 percent of his time. Musa became my "right-hand man". He translated PowerPoints for me, and did ongoing translation during workshops I facilitated and meetings I engaged in. Without him, the work I did for the MoPH to support them to develop their first strategic plan and build the capacity of internal teams to do planning would not have been possible.

After working with my strategic planning team for about a month, Dr. Sylvie asked if she could attend the initial capacity-building workshop I was facilitating with them. I replied, "Of course!" After the workshop, Dr. Sylvie informed me that she had a higher-level team of Afghans, all physicians with Master's degrees who spoke good English, as part of her project. She asked if they could attend future workshops I did for the Strategic Planning Team. I agreed and then asked whether her team could support us with consultations and larger workshops we were doing with different divisions across the Ministry, to which she approved. This partnership worked well as I trained Dr. Sylvie's team with mine in small group facilitation and other planning processes. For example, when we facilitated a national workshop to identify the strategic directions for the Ministry and key activities under each one, the more educated men and women from Dr. Sylvie's team verbally facilitated the small groups, while the original strategic planning team captured key ideas on flipcharts. Dr. Sylvie's team would then translate the group "discussion" into English and present their "work" in English in plenary which I could then provide feedback on. The approach was highly participatory so Ministry management and staff at a variety of levels would "own" the strategic plan that was co-created with them.

***

It was truly a gift to be working closely with Mustafa. He was someone who was so trusted and respected. High level teams including those from the World Bank and the IMF (International Monetary Fund) paraded through his office, and so I learned a lot as a "fly on the wall".

I remember one morning it started to snow watching the huge flakes drop gently out of the sky through the large office windows. Mustafa was observing them at the same time. I said, "As a child, I recall when it snowed like this sticking my tongue out and catching the falling flakes with my friends." Mustafa echoed, "So do I." It was a special moment.

I recall vividly my first day at the Ministry. I asked one of my co-workers where the women's washroom was. They showed me the door and said that this was the best one in that building. I entered unsure of what I would find. There were two stalls; one being a squat toilet/hole in the floor covered with ceramic with a water jug close by for washing; and a western toilet. Curiously, the squat toilet was quite clean, but the western toilet was filthy. I blanketed the seat with toilet paper and gingerly sat down. After doing my business I went to the sink to wash my hands. I was both surprised and rather horrified when water from inside the sink dripped down onto my shoes. I realized too late that the pipes were loose, enabling water to flow out of the sink and onto the floor.

I shared this experience with one of the Afghan women who I then saw reprimanding in Dari one of the male cleaners. The next time I used the washroom, the western toilet was much cleaner, and no water dripped onto my shoes.

Chapter 4

LIFE IN OUR COMPOUND

I love being in nature and being restricted to a small compound I felt like a bird in a cage. There were three Afghan guards with AK-47s at the perimeter of our compound. Some days after work I would pace around in circles inside the walls and felt a real need to move and be outdoors. I often thought the guards must be wondering what I was doing and why. We also had a well-equipped gym in one of the two houses so that helped many of us release stress and stay fit.

Kabul is situated in a bowl surrounded by mountains. Because there were few trees on the hills, often dust storms would come up; similar to those you see in old western movies. The poorer Afghans squatted on the hills surrounding Kabul and open sewers ran down the sides of the mountains. We didn't know all that we were breathing in. That said, my Canadian lungs didn't adjust well to the new environment, and I ended up being diagnosed with pneumonia twice within the first six months of being here.

When I first arrived in Kabul, there were eight consultants including myself in the compound. We were all working with different ministries. It was always a treat when we gathered for dinner around a long wooden table and shared stories of our day. I recall one forty-something consultant who was advising the Minister of Finance revealing that he wished he had paid more attention in Economics class at university, as now he was having to support the Minister in making high-level decisions such as whether to introduce VAT (a form of taxation) to bring more money into the Afghan government's coffers.

As we only got one day off per week, Friday, prayer day, Thursday nights were our weekends. We entertained ourselves in various ways.

I recall with fondness one night. We had a

campfire in the pit in front of one of the houses in our small compound. It was a beautiful clear night. The stars were illuminating the sky as there was little light pollution. One colleague brought marshmallows for all of us to roast that were so hard they must have been forgotten for six months or more in the back of his closet. He carved a few sticks for us and those who were adventurous enough to try, roasted the marshmallows over the open fire. At the same time, we shared stories of life back home, and whatever else came to mind. We laughed, joked and I felt so connected to the group and that moment. At such times I forgot where I was.

Another Thursday, Tom, the Colonel, brought out his guitar and as we sat round the campfire, he played many rock tunes we all knew and sang along to. Sometimes several people would get up and dance. There was so much camaraderie. Tom even had photocopied sheets with the words to many of the tunes. Sitting in a circle singing and dancing together, we forgot the stresses and uncertainty of being in a war zone and could have been anywhere on Earth.

One Friday we gave the cooks a break and Tom brought to the kitchen all the makings for sushi. His wife had sent him the wooden wrapping tools, special spices and all the fixings required. Someone put on a pot of rice.

We all gathered and made sushi and sashimi together all the while laughing and sharing stories from various parts of our lives. It was an evening I will never forget.

The house that was my "home" had a huge rooftop patio. It was a great place to hold parties. Consultants and people from the various embassies would sometimes rent our rooftop for going away parties and other special events. I recall one party where we had live music and various hors d'oeuvres. These get togethers were opportunities for us to connect with colleagues from a variety of backgrounds and cultures and forget about the fact we were working in a war zone.

The Canadian Ambassador seemed particularly interested in our project. He often invited us for lunch as well as to cocktail parties at the embassy. At the lunches he made a point of having me sit beside him and asking me how things were going, were there any challenges we were facing and how he might be of support. It was a great feeling to know that he cared.

One Friday afternoon we hosted a special event in our compound. It included local Afghans selling their wares such as beautiful Afghan women's clothing and paintings. We had delicious food and in the center of the lawn a traditional Afghan group was playing their melodious music. It was a beautiful day, and I recall feeling so happy and energized. The event attracted many colleagues from the various embassies and consultants from a variety of countries. It was unquestionably a success.

Afghanistan is a "dry" country. However, if you had access to a diplomatic pouch, you could have alcohol brought in regularly from various countries. The Colonel who lived in our compound had this perk. About every two months we would gather and give Tom our order for 6 bottles of red wine, 6 bottles of white, 24 beers or whatever we wished. A month or so after the shipment would arrive, and we would gleefully pick up our orders from Tom. You never knew what kind of wine or beer you would get. It could be a Cabernet Sauvignon from France or a Pinot Grigio from Spain. You just never knew. It was kind of fun not knowing.

I would keep my wine (as I prefer wine over beer) under my bed. I wonder what the cleaning ladies thought about us all having alcohol under our beds. On reflection, it seems a bit funny "hiding" alcohol under our beds in a Muslim country.

One highlight of my time in Kabul was doing yoga early in the morning with Anita, the Head of Mission. In the living room of her house in the compound she would set up her laptop, and we would do vinyasa flow yoga from 6 to 7. It was amazing to see the sun rising above one of the mountains that surrounded Kabul. It also felt so good to be doing something I would regularly do at home. Sharing that time with Anita was also memorable.

Another highlight was the yoga classes several women from the Canadian embassy taught on Friday afternoon. It was an opportunity not only to stretch and heal our bodies, but also to connect with women from a variety of backgrounds and cultures who were working in the various agencies.

Our Head of Mission loved being in nature. Although we had signed waivers that prevented us from walking in the street and resulting in us feeling caged in, Anita managed to convince the Head of Security to take us hiking outside of Kabul close to a big artificial lake, as long as our security folks stayed close by with the bulletproof vehicles. I remember the first time we hiked around the lake how amazing it felt. It was freeing and so amazing to be seeing another part of the country I had not seen.

One day we saw a family who had set up a carpet by the lake and were having a picnic. Their young boys were splashing in the lake. I asked if I could take their picture and to my amazement they said yes. That photo is a poignant reminder

TRUTHS AND CONTRADICTIONS

of those special Fridays when we got to escape from our compound.

During the initial months I worked in Kabul, consultants would come and go. One evening a female American consultant who had worked in many of the "Stan Countries" did not show up for dinner. Later we found out that she was trapped in a bunker underneath one of the buildings of an organization she was working with that had been attacked. She and over 100 others were crowded into this underground "safe" area that had space and toilets that ideally were for 50 people maximum. The only way she was able to communicate with our Head of Mission was by texting from her cell. I realized then and there that I needed to figure out how to text from my two, rather ancient flip phones, so that if I were in a similar situation, I would be able to communicate with the outside world. Nothing like adrenalin to get yourself moving!

One Thursday evening, the Head of Security shared that a Buzkashi event was happening the next day. I was feeling particularly unwell at the time, and thought I'd have a "lie in" on prayer day and perhaps a massage. I didn't feel much like going out. All my colleagues insisted that I didn't want to miss this special event which only happened about every eighteen months. That being the case I decided to join the others and was so glad I did.

After being searched for weapons, we were

escorted to "front row seats" on the bleachers which were close to the action. Buzkashi is a sport where two teams on horseback vie to grab a headless goat, take it from one end of the field and drop it inside a circle at the other end of the field. When this happens, the team scores a point. I found out that the man who scored the point often received up to $500 US from the warlord who was supporting his team. It was quite an experience. A number of times throughout the event it felt like the horses were coming right into the stands with us. I could see their flared nostrils and feel their warm breath on my face.

Later on, I found out that one of the warlords who had sponsored that Buzkashi event had been killed while in the receiving line at his daughter's wedding!

When I first arrived in Afghanistan we received detailed security information from our Head of Security. An example would be: "Two white Dodge Rams arrived in Kabul last night armed with IEDs (Improvised Explosive Devices). They plan to target the 'such and such' embassy on Friday at noon." This was a bit too much information for me. I preferred it later when we didn't get such detailed intelligence. Instead, we could be driving to work and the security person in the vehicle with us would say, we're taking an alternate route to the Ministry today. There is a group of protesters at the next traffic circle. They are currently peaceful but we're not sure if they may get violent.

A very scary thing that happened was one day when Finest, the grocery store we typically shopped at, was the scene of a suicide bomb attack. An entire family someone in the compound knew was shot and blown up in the attack. It was surreal.

Every time we drove by a large US army vehicle I would hold my breath. The US were known to be targets for having bombs strapped to their undercarriages. These could go off at any time. I realize on reflection how much stress I was living under while driving in the streets of Kabul. I met a man who was working as an independent contractor. The organization he was working for had hired a security person to always be by his side at a cost of $1200 US per day. Can you believe that! I have a picture of myself, this man, his security person and mine standing in front of a "bombed out" building and the shell of an old rusty Russian helicopter.

Chapter 5
GETTING DOWN TO BUSINESS

On day two at the Ministry, Mustafa took me to meet the Acting Minister of Public Health. She was a welcoming yet strong woman who gave me about forty-five minutes of her time. During our initial meeting she shared some background and issues she felt were important for me to know and understand. I underscored that I would be using participatory approaches to work with her people to create a 5-year strategic plan for the Ministry.

Initially, I met with the Minister quite often to update her on the project. Later, as she got increasingly busy, I met with one of her Deputies, Dr. Marlize, who strongly supported my work and often gave the opening address at workshops my team and I facilitated.

During my initial meeting with the Minister, she surprised me with the following "You are aware that initially we were going to hire a policy person as well as someone with planning expertise. Since you have a background in both, we've decided we don't need a policy person, at least not right now, we feel you can do both roles." Then the Minister added, "I would like a report from you within a month, with your recommendations on how we can improve policy and planning processes within the Ministry." In that moment, I thought—*policy AND planning? How was I going to develop a strategic plan with the Ministry using participatory processes, build the capacity of internal teams in nine months, and also do policy work?*

I went back to my office pondering what would be my next step. I asked the policy person whose desk was beside mine whether he had an organizational chart of the Ministry in English. He said no, but he had one in the local language and printed it out for me. I then looked at the fifteen boxes below the Minister and Deputies, and proceeded to ask which department was which and who was the head of each one writing in English beside each box. Then I asked Aarash if he would take me to each department, introduce me to each Director, whereupon I would ask for about one hour of their time. One by one Aarash did that, and in the process explained that I would like one hour of their time within the next couple of days to interview them to better understand their policy and planning processes, as well as what was working, what wasn't and their recommendations to improve current processes. Within a month I had interviewed the top fifteen managers within the Ministry, rolled up the findings of those interviews and added my own recommendations to theirs. I presented the report to the Minister. This proved to be a useful strategy as I now had had one-on-one time with each manager and in the future when any of them (mainly men) asked why was such and such done, I would state, "Remember the interviews I did with you all last fall, based on what you told me you needed and wanted. That is why we did what we did."

As mentioned, part of my mandate was to hold workshops with my team. I taught them to facilitate small groups which were used to consult with representatives from the seven divisions across the Ministry toward development of the strategic plan, and to facilitate capacity building workshops related to the new operational planning tools we had developed.

We were planning a training workshop for more than one hundred Ministry staff and there were no training rooms at the Ministry compound that could accommodate that number. The Head of the strategic planning team informed me that one hospital had a large training room that would "fit the bill". He made an appointment, and we drove together to meet the doctor who was head of the hospital to enquire about its availability. He invited us into his office, asked for tea and biscuits to be served and went about small talk. I was anxious to get to the point, the reason we were there. I couldn't help but be distracted by a show that was playing on a TV mounted close to the ceiling in my line of vision. There was a bevy of Persian-like women with diaphanous pants, bejewelled tops and bare midriffs dancing provocatively around the room. The volume was turned down, but I could hear alluring music playing in the background. I had never witnessed anything quite like this in all of my professional life in Muslim countries. After this initial distraction, I was able to engage with Dr. I. He had his secretary check the dates for availability and he agreed to have us use the facility. I was so relieved when we got back into our Toyota Land Cruiser and headed back to the Ministry.

Before we left, I asked whether we could see the room and the washrooms. The training room was perfect, but the washrooms left a lot to be desired. They were filthy. I asked to check the men's as well as the women's and found that the men's washroom was cleaner. I told the Director of the hospital that we would appreciate the women's and men's washrooms being well cleaned the morning our workshop was to begin.

Facilitating training workshops in a country like Afghanistan is not for the faint of heart. I learned quickly after our first workshop that we not only had to design and plan the workshop, create and organize the training materials, but also provide the food and water, organize to have it delivered, bring toilet paper and soap for the washrooms, and in some cases provide transportation to participants.

One training experience that is indelibly etched in my mind was when the team and I were facilitating a workshop at a hospital that had a large conference room about forty-five minutes from the Ministry. We started off as planned. I was impressed by how well each member of the team was doing with their presentations. I was sitting at the front beside several of my team members while another was speaking to the larger group when suddenly a number of cell phones went off. My two cells (I had two in case one of the two cell towers went down) were on the stage out of reach so I whispered softly to Aarash, the team member who was sitting beside me, "Something must be going on."

The next moment a woman who was Head of Pharmacy stood up and screamed "The Ministry of Public Health is being attacked." I knew I had to hold the room. I stood up and said "I understand that you are afraid. It is scary for me as well. This kind of thing does not happen in Canada. But listen…" you could have heard a pin drop, "… we are safe here. If you choose to leave, feel free to do so; however, we will finish the workshop." The woman sat down. No one left and we finished the workshop. Later, I found out that the US embassy which was right beside the Ministry had been attacked. Somehow snipers had gotten inside the gates, climbed the scaffolding that was being used to build a new Marriott hotel inside their compound, perched on top and were shooting around the compound. They were also firing mortars. Because they were so close to the Ministry, some of the bullets and mortars had entered that compound, having ricocheted off the walls. The Ministry of Public Health had not been the object of attack but had suffered collateral damage.

We found out later that two of our colleagues had been stuck in their offices and unable to escape the Ministry. Thankfully no one was injured.

Later that evening reflecting on the day, I wondered how I had in the moment had the courage to stand up and hold the room. I am a petite woman, less than five foot two, so my size was not a factor. I guess I felt a responsibility to prevent chaos in the room and a potential stampede as there were more than one hundred people present. The next day, day two of our workshop, I was told by my Head of Security that I was unable to attend as the risk was too great. I later learned that seventy-five percent of the Ministry participants had attended and all of my team showed up and did their part in finishing the training. I was so proud of them all. It was another day in the life of an international consultant in Afghanistan.

Another time, the team and I were facilitating

a training workshop in the local language. At this point I was more of a resource person having trained the team in facilitation and strategic and operational planning. One fellow on the team had not prepared and we all noticed it when he got up to speak and shared his part of the presentation. It was awful! I felt so disappointed and angry at the same time. How could he have not pulled his weight and let down the team? During the debrief I was seething inside. I asked the team how they felt things went; what had worked well, if there were any concerns, and how we could have done better. The one team member acknowledged he could have done better. I invited others to share how it had influenced them until I no longer could hold my anger and frustration. I more or less reamed out the said team member and shared how his behavior made me feel and how disappointed I was that we hadn't all given it our best. Suddenly, tears streamed down my face, and I realized I was crying. The team, largely Muslim Afghan men, didn't know what to do with me. With distraught looks on their faces they said, "It's okay Ms. Minerva. We'll do better next time."

Another unique aspect of the work day was that driving to work was always an experience. You never knew whether your vehicle would be stopped by the military police and papers demanded from your driver. One week, three out of five days my vehicle was stopped. We soon learned that President Karzai had passed a law prohibiting private security firms to be transporting foreigners in the country. He wanted his own people to take over that role. Although the correct paperwork had been submitted to the appropriate ministry along with the requested funds, the documents were apparently being held on someone's desk and had not been processed. Often when we were stopped, the driver would negotiate for a while and then would have to go to a local police station and pay seventy-five US dollars to continue driving the vehicle.

Chapter 6
A MEMORABLE LUNCH HOUR

Farzanah and I often would eat lunch outdoors in the rose garden of the Ministry. I use the term "rose garden" loosely as the roses were often covered with dust and through their very existence were reminders of the resilience of the Afghan people. How they survived in this rather unfriendly environment was amazing!

Farzanah and I would share our respective lunches and delighted in learning more about each other and sampling food from one another's "kitchens". Farzanah had a mother who was very ill. She was the eldest of four girls and had one brother. Not having the long-term care system that we have in Canada, Farzanah and her family shared the task of caring for their mother. They all had full-time jobs, yet they had a schedule and took turns going home at lunch to feed, bathe, and move their mother. I was amazed at how lovingly Farzanah spoke about her family. She and her three sisters were all medical doctors with master's degrees. Her youngest sister, Zahra, was a Fulbright scholar. They were all beautiful women from the inside out.

One afternoon Farzanah and I were sharing our lunch. I was perched on one of the metal, not so comfortable, benches in the garden. Each time we sat together, we shared personal stories, and I learned more and more about Farzanah and her family.

Suddenly, out of the blue, a deafening explosion cut through the air. I had never experienced anything like it. Farzanah immediately got on her cell phone and called each one of her siblings to make sure they were all okay. Reflecting on this later, I realized she had been doing this for the last fifteen or so years. Each time a mortar or bomb went off Farzanah would get in touch with each family member to ensure they were okay.

I was getting texts from my Head of Security. They read: "Stay where you are. There's been a suicide bomb attack at the military hospital across the road from the Ministry. We still don't know how many casualties there are." Later I learned that five or six suicide bombers had entered the hospital emergency and killed a number of Afghan patients, their families and physicians. *How could fellow Afghans kill their own people in a hospital of all places? What would compel them to commit such a heinous act?*

Back to the rose garden. After a few hours, the bulletproof vehicle with my Afghan driver

TRUTHS AND CONTRADICTIONS

appeared at the Ministry to take me back to the compound. The drive that usually took no more than thirty minutes took about one and a half hours. There was chaos in the streets. People and vehicles were everywhere.

At dinner that night I felt quiet and a bit numb. I had not really believed what I had experienced earlier that day. The sound of that incredible explosion indelibly etched in my brain. How could anyone get used to this? I realized Farzanah and her peers and family had been living with war for about thirty years. *How could anyone adapt to this uncertainty, violence, and senseless killing?*

I started to reflect on the Afghans I was working with and the stories of their lives that bit by bit they were sharing with me. So many had been close to death. Many of them had lost family and friends through this senseless violence. *Why had a number of them left the country when the war was at its peak and returned when there was peace, to rebuild and start again? What lessons could we learn from these people about living with uncertainty, keeping our hearts open and compassionate, rather than having our hearts turn to stone and fill with fear and hatred?* The men and women with whom I worked showed kindness, caring, understanding and a passion to make a positive difference in the world.

I later learned about Madrasahs, which are

religious schools that taught reading and writing and made each student mindlessly repeat passages from the Quran daily, rocking back and forth while doing so. There was no critical thinking taught at these schools. The Taliban and other fundamentalist Muslim leaders indoctrinated boys from a young age so they would carry out anything they were told to do in the name of Allah. Boys of such young ages as 11 and 12 were told to strap on bombs and be suicide bombers killing foreigners and their own kind. Their parents, being illiterate, thought they were doing their sons a favor by enrolling them in these religious schools. They had no idea what their children were being taught and how their lives would end.

The sadness I feel for these young boys and their parents is hard to express. My heart cracks open for these poor souls. I feel intense anger at how religion can be used in such self-serving and harmful ways. Religion is meant to teach love, caring and compassion for one another. How have so many of our religions become mechanisms of control and hatred, turning people into puppets on strings with the religious leaders being the powerful and controlling puppeteers?

While working in Pakistan a few years before, I recall meeting a consultant who worked throughout Muslim countries in Asia and Africa, telling me how he had witnessed traditional Saudi

TRUTHS AND CONTRADICTIONS

Islam strategically infiltrating many of those countries he visited. I witnessed the difference on a recent visit to Turkey that twelve years previously had been relatively open. At that time, I saw no women in burkas or covered in black from head to toe but now they seemed to be everywhere. It was happening! Sadness and anger flood my veins when I think of it and its negative impact on women and girls.

Frequently, when I walked through the halls of the Ministry, women of all ages, often dressed in black from head to toe, would hug and kiss me three times on both cheeks (which is the custom in Afghanistan when greeting people you care about), and repeat words in Dari that I didn't understand. I was told that they were thanking and blessing me for the work I was doing for their country. The first time it happened I felt tears well up and it was all I could do to keep them from running down my cheeks. One day Farzanah said to me, "How can it be that you have only been here three months, and everyone seems to know you?" Perhaps it's because I was a western woman, who although dressed in Afghan tops and scarves, still was not a typical person for them to encounter?

Chapter 7
INTERESTING CHARACTERS

Conflict zones attract interesting people. Everyone has a story or multiple stories that are so different from friends and family at home. There is something so juicy about living and working with people who crave and thrive on a sense of adventure.

One such character was one of our Heads of Security, Chris. At one time he had worked as Angelina Jolie's personal bodyguard. Another time he was a security person on boats off Senegal to protect them from the many pirates that patrolled those waters. It was crazy to hear that he was unable to use any weapons as part of this job. He could only use water cannons and his own brute force if and when pirates tried to board the ships he was protecting. I couldn't imagine putting yourself at such risk.

Our other Head of Security, Kenneth, was originally from England. At one point he packed up his life and headed for Thailand. He ended up meeting a special Thai woman who became his partner. To help support her and to keep her busy while he was travelling the world for work, he bought her a car wash. An interesting feature of this car wash was that it also had a massage parlor beside it. Picture how awesome it would be to get a massage while your car was being washed! How creative and entrepreneurial!

Another feature of life overseas is embassy parties. They give you the opportunity to not only meet women and men from your own embassy but also from others.

I recall one evening chatting with the Head of Development from the Canadian embassy. The conversation got around to me asking her how she began working in a conflict zone. She told me the story of getting divorced while living in Ottawa and working with Foreign Affairs. She noted that the circle she hung out with was very small, and everyone "knew your business". She wanted to escape to a place where no one knew her and where she could start again. She went to Iraq, then Iran and now Afghanistan. Now she was "labelled" as a conflict-zone person, so she kept being assigned missions in war zones. I was happy to hear when she left that she was named Ambassador to Bangladesh which was NOT a war zone.

It seemed that many of the people I met and engaged in conversation with were escaping a certain situation or life event. They also wanted to inject more excitement and adventure into their lives.

Chapter 8
CHRISTMAS HOLIDAYS

I was so looking forward to heading home for Christmas. I had negotiated a fly back as part of the contract discussions within three months of being in Afghanistan. Normally you had to work for six months before getting to fly back home. I told the hiring team that Christmas was extremely important to me and my family, and that was a condition of me accepting the consultancy. They agreed with the caveat that if I did not work for six months in-country, that I would have to reimburse them for the fly back. I knew that wouldn't be a problem because once I commit, I follow through.

Before leaving, one of the cooks with a young child who got frequent bouts of bronchitis asked if when I returned home, I could purchase some pediatric cough syrup for him. He understood the cough syrup we had in Canada was of better quality than what they sold in Afghanistan. I happily fulfilled his request.

I arrived home so happy to see my sweet David and have his big strong arms wrap around me. I so missed his affection and our intimacy. I immediately got wrapped up in Christmas preparations, and finally after cleaning up after our Christmas dinner felt like I was crashing. I realized I was bone tired, so I went to bed and slept about thirteen hours. On awakening I was still tired yet I wanted to see my friends and connect more with family who were close by. A couple of days later, despite more than twelve hours sleep each night, I was dragging around and having some shortness of breath. It was New Year's Eve, and David encouraged me to go to a walk-in clinic in a nearby town that happened to be open. The physician upon listening to my chest suspected pneumonia, ordered a chest x-ray and prescribed an antibiotic. Within several days his diagnosis was confirmed. Soon after I had to return to Afghanistan.

Many of my friends were curious about how I could live and work in a war zone without being on "high alert" all the time. I told them that doing yoga each morning, meditating, and connecting with my Sweetie were key strategies I used. Sleeping in on my day off and having regular massages were also helpful. I realized that rarely did my body go into high alert. I guess I so believed in the work I was doing and felt so passionate about it that, most of the time, I was able to keep my amygdala (part of the brain)

TRUTHS AND CONTRADICTIONS

from revving up and causing stress hormones to be released throughout my body, sending me into fight, flight, or freeze. The only times I recall feeling wired was when the suicide bombers attacked the military hospital across the road from the Ministry, and when a colleague was trapped in a bunker at another facility.

Chapter 9

BACK IN THE SADDLE

On my return to Kabul, I got back into working incredible hours. Getting up many days at 6 am so I could do one hour of yoga with our Head of Mission, skype with David, and have breakfast before heading to the Ministry at about 8:30 am. I would leave the office at about 4 pm, go for a walk around the compound or perhaps the gym to work out, and then after dinner work often till 9 or 10 pm, keeping up this pace for six days a week. Within several more months I got pneumonia yet again.

Fortunately, there was a German clinic with excellent medical staff that many ex-pats frequented. I found out the reason pneumonia was so prevalent was because of all the nasty things we were breathing in including dust, as the mountains around Kabul are deforested and dust storms are frequent. Also, because there are many squatters on the hills surrounding Kabul, and there are open sewers running down the outside of those hills resulting in you breathing e-coli and who knows what else.

After facilitating a number of consultation sessions across each division of the Ministry with my strategic planning team, we hosted a national workshop. The aim was to develop the strategic directions for the Ministry for the next five years, identify some key activities under each one and gain agreement on the mission and vision. On the day of the workshop, I awoke and realized that I was losing my voice. While skyping with my husband I felt it getting scratchier and scratchier. I remember feeling stressed on my way to the Ministry. *How would I act as chief facilitator if I was unable to speak?* Other questions circled in my head such as *Would the process I'd used to develop a strategic plan in North America work here? Will my team do a good job facilitating the small groups?*

When I arrived at the workshop venue, I took several deep breaths to calm and ground myself and found out that one of my team who was to facilitate a small group, was ill. That meant in addition to being chief facilitator that I would also need to facilitate his small group. I offered up a prayer that my voice would return. After drinking a cup of warm tea, miraculously my voice began to improve. I managed to make it through the day, at first sounding a bit croaky, and was able to do what was needed.

The Minister attended the workshop, and I was amazed at how "hands off" she was. It was clear she was interested in what "her people" had to say. When I gathered with the team to debrief after the workshop, all of them were beaming. They felt elated about how they had all performed and the consensus we had reached on the key elements of the strategic plan. I praised them all for a job well done.

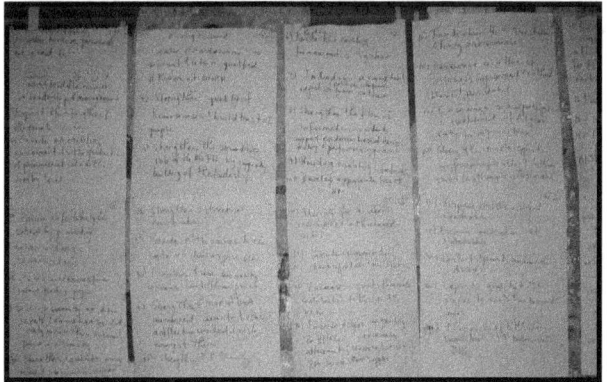

*Flip charts on the wall at the national conference

I recall one week when three out of five days, my vehicle, while heading to work, was stopped by the police. One of those times, the information my Afghan driver gave to the policeman and the paperwork he showed him, did not satisfy the officer. He said that we had to go to a nearby police station and pay a fine. I immediately got on one of my two cell phones (if one cell tower went down, I would be able to connect with another) and called my Head of Security, Chris, and apprised him of the situation. He said I had two options. I could go with the driver to the police station and stay there for who knows how long, or ride in the soft skin vehicle that drove behind the bullet proof one I was riding in with the three guys armed with AK-47s and go to work with them. I chose the latter. I recall bombing through the streets of Kabul, the wind brushing my cheeks, my hair flying, squeezed in between the three guards with AK-47s feeling like I was in a war movie. It was a bit surreal. I did get to the Ministry in one piece thankfully and that never happened again!

I said at the outset I thrive on adventure. At times like these, I really wondered how much more adventure I needed!

As part of the planning process, a senior management team was created to enable them to "feed into the process". That said, they primarily assisted with the development of the performance measurement framework for the 5-year plan. Key representatives from donors of the Ministry, as well as senior Ministry officials, were part of this group. After the draft strategic plan was shared with this team, it then began its journey through the various policy layers. Initially we presented it to a technical working group composed of a number of nongovernmental organizations (NGOs). I was shocked when the two representatives of the World Bank who were part of our committee, stood up and poked holes in what we had created. They had been part of the development process. If they felt so strongly about certain parts of it, why hadn't they voiced their concerns during the development process?

After that meeting it was clearer why these men had done what they did. Some World Bank representatives who had recently arrived in-country had read the strategic plan. In a document submitted to the Head of Policy and Planning, they questioned and challenged a number of items and recommended certain things be changed. I was livid. Their comments included reducing the number of strategic directions and changing how they were written. They ripped holes in something that had taken months to create through collaborative processes and using words and phrases that the co-creators owned.

It was clear the World Bank representatives had little or no understanding of collaborative processes and co-creating strategies and documents, including the importance of using the language of those who contributed to their development. In a meeting with two senior Ministry officials, I was asked to respond to each comment that was contained in the World Bank's critique of our strategic plan. I was able to address all the points this group had raised citing evidence from different parts of the document, and fortunately had to change little in the plan. That said, it was frustrating and created extra work to address their concerns. The comments of the World Bank representatives were academic without full understanding or consideration of their implementation.

While nearing the end of my nine-month contract, I was informed that the strategic planning team had requested that my contract be extended. After some consideration and discussions with my Head of Mission, the donor and my husband, I agreed to another four months on the condition that I have four weeks of vacation and that my husband be able to visit and stay with me in the compound for a short while.

Chapter 10
LAST DAYS OF MISSION #1

At the end of my first mission, I wanted to treat Farzanah to a luncheon. She told me that her youngest sister had just returned from America where she was studying and she had just completed her Master's Degree. Farzanah asked whether her sister could also accompany us. I agreed and asked her where she would like to go to lunch. Farzanah chose an Afghan restaurant that our security folks would not normally allow us to go to. After scoping out the restaurant, Kenneth agreed that I could go there as long as one of our Afghan guards came with us. I was told not to acknowledge him and that he would be sitting some distance away from us in the restaurant.

When we entered the restaurant, I noticed that I was the only foreigner in sight. The ceilings were decorated with beautiful flowing material. Farzanah chose a table in the corner away from the crowd. As we moved toward the table I looked around and realized there were Taliban eating in the same establishment. I knew them by their traditional clothes, long beards, and turbaned heads. I tried to be nonchalant, but in my mind wondered what am I doing here? I asked Farzanah and her sister what they would like to order. They were excited to introduce me to some Afghan foods they really enjoyed. First up were various types of meat on long brass skewers. Rice and various types of vegetables followed. I was so full at the end of the meal. I rarely eat red meat, but so as to not disappoint, I tried every one of the dishes.

At the luncheon I found out that Farzanah's sister, Zahra, had returned to Kabul from the US to support her sisters and brother in caring for their mother who was bedridden at the family home. Zahra really wanted to stay in the US and do her doctorate, but family duty called. At that moment, I realized how strong family values were among Afghans. Such love and commitment.

The day before my departure, while cruising through the streets of Kabul, I saw some young boys riding on a donkey. Kenneth, the Head of Security, said he would let me out of the vehicle so I could ride a donkey if I wished. I declined this offer. Soon after, I saw a group of young boys playing cricket and asked Kenneth if I could go and play with them. To my astonishment he said yes. I have not much idea about how to play cricket, but I went to bat several times and have some photos of myself with a group of smiling young boys who I would say were about 12 years of age. Me with my head scarf billowing in the wind smiling from ear to ear. It was a special moment captured digitally.

Two Muslim cleaning ladies cleaned my room on a regular basis. They were dressed in black from head to toe, but their faces were not covered. Initially I smiled at them, but we had no way to communicate verbally, them speaking Dari and me English. Bit by bit we became closer communicating through smiles and gestures. Then came the day when one of them gave me a huge bear hug and lifted me right off the floor. I giggled and imagined I was smiling ear to ear. From that day forward that was how this woman greeted me. We had this unusual yet special bond.

I had a framed photo of myself with my son and daughter on the bookshelf in my room. The friendly cleaner asked through gestures whether she could have that picture. I took it out of the frame and gave it to her and could feel her heart opening with gratitude. I was happy she felt that way. I also gave her some boots and other clothing I had as there was no way I could take back everything I had brought and more, plus I knew she would really appreciate these things.

The evening before leaving Afghanistan, I invited Mustafa, Farzanah and Aarash for dinner at our compound. Sadly, Farzanah could not attend because as a single woman she could not venture out at night without a male relative.

During dinner, Mustafa shared how he was kidnapped by the Taliban and held hostage for nine days. He described how the Taliban stormed into the office of the foreign NGO he was working for, grabbed some videos that were produced in Europe and some bottles, and accused Mustafa and several of his colleagues of drinking alcohol and watching forbidden media.

Mustafa's head was covered in a black hood. He was taken by truck to an unknown residence and held hostage in the basement for nine days. Suddenly, on day nine Mustafa was released unexpectedly and allowed to go home. Within twenty-four hours he was on a bus headed for Pakistan. He told his wife and family he was no longer safe in Afghanistan and that when he found a place for them to live, he would send for them. That is what he did. Mustafa and his family spent a number of years in Pakistan where he worked for another NGO that served the border of Pakistan and Afghanistan.

The morning of my departure finally arrived. I remember that day vividly. My feelings were bittersweet. I had connected with a number of Afghans and foreign consultants alike and felt that I had made some sort of positive difference. I would miss the excitement and camaraderie yet was excited to be returning home, reconnecting with family and friends, and settling back into my "other" life.

At Kabul airport, I initially went into a curtained small room and was padded down by a Muslim woman security guard dressed in black from head to toe, while my luggage went through the security screening. I then lined up at the airline check-in desk and patiently waited to get my boarding pass and have my luggage ticketed. As I was leaving the check-in counter a young Afghan man with a stern face and gruff voice called out to me. He said, "Show me your papers." I played dumb and responded, "I don't know what you're talking about. I have my passport," which I handed to him. "I've been working to support your Ministry of Health and am now heading home."

He insisted, "Call the organization you are working with. You will NOT be leaving today. You need those papers before you can leave the country."

My heart was pounding while being interrogated by this Afghan official. I knew the papers he was speaking about. When I initially arrived in the country our Head of Operations took me to a government office where we paid seventy-five US dollars and received papers that enabled me to work in-country. For a while, these papers hadn't been asked for and so they were not renewed. I am not a good liar and while I was feeling threatened on the inside, I focused on appearing strong and composed on the outside.

I observed another young Afghan male sitting down behind this aggressive man who was speaking to me. He had a kind face. I looked at him, at the same time appealing for his colleague to let me pass. The man who was seated exchanged a few words in the local language with his workmate and the stern-faced man said, "Well I guess you can go this time."

As I moved through security, which seemed to take forever, I felt ill at ease, hoping that I would not be stopped. Next came a booth and a customs official who in addition to asking a number of questions, finger-printed me. Apparently, a new technology had been introduced into Afghanistan and now I was in an international database—great! When I finally reached the waiting area, I phoned my Head of Security and told him what had happened. I said, "I almost was not allowed to leave the country as I didn't have those Internal documents. Please make sure all the consultants get them as they are now required."

I was so happy and relieved to board that plane and fly towards home. I was so looking forward to arriving home and having David hold me in his big strong arms. While on the airplane I reflected on a number of things many of us take for granted living in the western world.

They included:

• *Freedom:* The freedom to walk in the streets and in nature. In Afghanistan, I travelled in a bulletproof vehicle with a personal bodyguard who was armed with a pistol and an AK-47. I was unable to walk in the streets. On the rare occasion (such as on the outskirts of Kabul on prayer day), I was able to walk outside with my armed and flak jacketed bodyguard by my side.

• *Electricity, heat and light:* Recently the electricity was out for two days at the Ministry of Public Health where I was working. I interviewed a number of people in a cold portable with the doors wide open and got chilled to the bone.

• *Internet connectivity:* When the electricity has challenges, the ability to connect with the internet is compromised. I kept in touch via Skype with family and friends and when I had no internet I was negatively affected by the lack of connection.

• *Clean and fresh air:* As Kabul is in a bowl, surrounded by mountains that are deforested, there is a large amount of dust in the air, which gets into your lungs.

Also, a number of squatters have built their homes on the edge of the mountains and there are open sewers. Therefore you breathe in e-coli and who knows what else! Many people who work in Afghanistan get what's called the "Kabul cough".

• *Clean water:* In Afghanistan as in many developing countries, it is not safe to drink from the tap or to brush your teeth with tap water. It's recommended to use bottled water.

• *The ability to dress how I choose:* In Afghanistan, even as a foreigner it is important to respect the culture, so I always wore a headscarf and was well covered (usually with a long jacket and long skirt or pants). When it gets hot it is challenging to stay cool when you're all wrapped up. I don't know how those women in burkas do it!

Chapter 11
HEADING HOME AND RE-ENTRY

The first leg of my trip home was with Aeroflot and that was an experience! The first thing I noticed was that flies were flitting about the cabin. The next was the thin cushions, if you could call them that, covering the metal seats that were not at all comfortable. The plane clearly was old and had not been refurbished.

Soon after boarding, a family with two children appeared. After some harsh words they were told to go to a different part of the plane where the family would be separated. There were a number of empty seats in front of where I was sitting that would accommodate them altogether. I spoke up to one of the flight attendants commenting that there were seats in front of me where the whole family could sit. The initial response was "No, they had not paid for that class of seats." Looking at the seats they didn't look any different from the one I was sitting in. I pressed my point and begrudgingly the flight attendant changed her tune and acquiesced to having the family sit together where I had suggested.

Not long after we took off, I smelled smoke coming from the curtained galley. Would you believe several of the flight attendants were smoking while preparing the food? I was never so happy to get off a flight as that one!

After that trip I vowed NEVER to fly Aeroflot again.

I was so excited to return home. I was looking forward to seeing my husband, my family, and friends. As one of my sisters lived in Ottawa, I was able to break up my trip and stay with her and her family for several days. Not long after my arrival we were watching the 11 o'clock news. Suddenly, a story about Afghanistan flashed across the screen. In it a hotel was being attacked. Men were dropping from helicopters onto the roof and throwing grenades and IEDs. Flames were licking various sections of the roof as they dropped. My sister, noting that it was a hotel in Kabul, asked if I knew of it. I was flabbergasted to realize that yes, it was the Intercontinental Hotel, the one that I had facilitated a workshop with my team at several months before. How was this hotel being infiltrated? It was up on a hill with a gate and security you had to pass through to enter with security similar to that used for screening at airports. Later I learned that the attack was quickly contained and fortunately not a lot of the hotel had been damaged or lives lost. It was sobering.

TRUTHS AND CONTRADICTIONS

Made me realize how at risk we all are working in places like Afghanistan. I was so sad to hear that a few months later, the Serena Hotel in Kabul had been attacked and a number of humanitarian workers, including several Canadians, had been killed.

Chapter 12
DEEPENING MY UNDERSTANDING

I am curious by nature and love history. My "why" in writing this book is to dispel myths about Afghans, Afghanistan, and Islam, and to help the reader understand the amazing resilience, courage, and humanitarian focus of many of the Afghan people. My larger mission is to help build peace and understanding because when we are curious and seek to understand, I believe there can be no war or open conflict.

While in Afghanistan I worked long hours and did not have a lot of time for social chit-chat with my strategic planning team or to do much research on the country and its history.

After my mission, I kept in touch virtually with a few people, and interviewed some, eager to learn more about their experiences of growing up in Afghanistan. I also was curious to learn about key historical events such as when the Taliban took the country the first time, when the Russians invaded, when the Taliban took the country the second time, and how these events impacted their lives.

More recently I did some online research to learn even more. I share the information I gathered from these interviews and research so you can see a different vision of Afghans, Afghanistan, and Islam, and become curious yourself in the hope to bring more peace and understanding to this subject and to the world.

Growing Up in Afghanistan

My team ranges in age from 45 to 67 years. A number of them were born outside of Kabul. Many spent their early years in rural villages. Nearly all of them have lived in other countries as their families chose to flee during the Soviet invasion and/or when the Taliban took the country in 1996. Many spent those years in Pakistan and/or Iran, so their education was disrupted. Some, more recently, did graduate degrees abroad.

It is amazing to me, how after so much strife and upheaval, they all returned to Afghanistan and participated in trying to rebuild and develop the country into one that respects human rights, and values peace and education for all.

Benesh shared:

"From childhood I liked school. I was very happy to go to school at age 5. We had a good life until age 11. My father supported us to go to school and I was always in first position. He was so proud of me. In grade 6 my father went to a remote area for work. He went by horse and fell from a bridge into a river and died. We never saw my father's body. I had to play the role of fathering my family. My mother was only 28 and had seven children; the last one born six months after my father passed. I worked hard to support my brothers and sisters and worked hard to support myself. ... I focused on having a good education. My life story was about taking care of the family."

Zahra recalled:

"From birth to age 10 we lived in my uncle's place, and we all had our own rooms and space. It had a big yard with a grapevine and a well inside. In winter it was full of snow and in summer full of green with a garden. ... Later I recall my father listening to the BBC with a low volume. There was overall political tension. ... We were middle income. Being rich at that time was a threat to the Communists."

Mirwais shared:

"I lived in a place where there were constant challenges throughout my life. In very early childhood the Soviets were in Afghanistan. There was fighting between the Soviets and Mujahideen (Afghan resistance fighters). The Mujahideen would shell rockets at the Soviet outposts. Sometimes there would be an alarm at school. We had to leave as soon as possible and run home. Often the shelling started before I got home. Then the civil war began."

Parwais shared:

"When I was a small child, we had sheep and goats. I used to go with my dad and other siblings to take care of those animals. There were negative feelings about the Russians. … My childhood was complicated and full of trauma. Mother was a housewife [and] uneducated. Father was a farmer (literate) and studied reading and writing at the mosque. … I was a change agent from a young age. I challenged things. Even religious beliefs and practices."

Shahmeer recalled:

"We were living in a peaceful village. My father was doing minor surgeries. It was difficult to work in Kabul; under the Communist regime it was a challenge. … We had a simple, joyful life. We had sheep and cows. My brother and I helped with them. We started to go to a nearby mosque to learn how to read and write. You tend to go to the mosque around age 4 and at age 7 you attend first grade."

Amina shared:

"My family moved to Pakistan when I was three. ... We moved back to Afghanistan in 2001 when my family heard the Taliban was removed from Afghanistan by the US. I started grade 6 in Kabul. It was very different because I had been studying at a Pakistani school and was used to Urdu. It was difficult for me to understand Dari and Pashtu. It was a big challenge for me writing in Dari and Pashtu. I suffered with the new environment. There was not such a good structure. It was a bit disorganized when the schools reopened. But later things became beautiful. I made new friends. My teachers and father supported me. I got the basic education I wanted and needed."

Marlize recalled:

"I had a very happy childhood to age 12, from a well-educated family with a reasonable lifestyle. My mother and father were well educated, and education was so important in my family. My siblings and

I were always top of our class at school.

"When the war started everything changed. Each day became tougher and tougher. Schools shut down so I studied at home at age 12 with my mother's help. The government announced that children could take an exam and if they passed, they could skip a grade. I studied two years in one at home. My aunt came and brought me to Kabul where I started grade 8. It was a great success. After the last exam I came back to my province and enrolled in year 9 (three months late). I passed my mid-year at the end of the year and the end of the year exam after three months. … Education was an important part of my life. My dream was to become a doctor.

"In grade 9 the security became worse. Our relatives had guns to protect us. … I was shivering at night when I heard a leaf blow. My parents said, if you see something or someone enters the house just call us.

"In grade 12 the security became very difficult. All night there was fighting. There was no authorized government and lots of robbery. My father had a pistol for hunting birds. I had to guard the petrol with my sister. At 4 am [it] was my turn. We shared this with my father and mother. We each had two hours to guard the petrol. When our house was hit by two rockets (when the Mujahideen fought against the government) that is when we finally decided to leave."

Farzanah contributed:

"We travelled a lot during the golden years (1970s) and had no fear of travelling. People were afraid of the police and army and respected them. People respected rules and regulations. Kabul was a well-organized, beautiful, clean city. We even had female bus drivers at that time. During the national holiday celebrations, we went to the desert or the mountains for picnics. Women had the freedom to wear anything they wished to wear. Kabul used to be a giant garden."

Farzaad shared:

"I did my primary school in Kabul. It was an enjoyable life. We were playing football and local games. The first day of school I remember my grandfather took me to school with my four cousins. I was very happy to go to school and enjoyed it. The quality of education was high at that time. … My first teacher was my teacher for four years. I am still connected with her. We had such a strong bond with our teachers. At that time there were no private schools. … After the civil war [after 1992], children never enjoyed the same quality of education as we enjoyed before that."

Asadi shared:

"I was born by the side of a lively river and at the foot of the mountains, where I spent my early years. In our village, people cared deeply for one another and always shared in each other's happiness and sadness. The government wasn't very strong, but that didn't matter much because people took care of their own problems and kept their area safe. Back then, everyone felt proud, happy, and free."

In addition to interviewing my team about their experiences growing up in Afghanistan, I was keen to learn what their experiences had been related to key historic events.

Below is a timeline of key historical events so you can better understand the context.

TRUTHS AND CONTRADICTIONS
Key Historical Dates For Afghanistan From The Early 1900s To Present Day

- 1919-1929 – King Amanullah reigned; the position of women improved during his reign.
- 1929-1933 – Muhammad Nadir Shah came into power, forced Amanullah's exile; closed schools to girls, women again had to be veiled; many other reforms were repealed.
- 1933 – Muhammad Nadir Shah was assassinated.
- 1933-1973 – King Zahir Shah and his cousin Daoud Khan set a reformist course for the country. The Afghan government enlisted foreign advisors, established girls' schools and later instituted a new constitution that granted Afghan women the right to vote. In urban areas women attended college, took jobs outside the home, ran businesses and even ventured into politics. Kabul became cosmopolitan.
- The 1960s and 1970s were Afghanistan's "glory days". Kabul was a cosmopolitan city where women attended university and wore mini-skirts and stockings.
- 1973 – King Zahir Shah was overthrown

in a coup and Mohammad Daoud Khan declared himself President
- 1978 April – Military units loyal to the Marxist People's Democratic Party of Afghanistan (PDPA) killed President Mohammad Daoud Khan and his family and installed its leader Nur Muhammad Taraki as President.
- 1978-1992 – Afghan Civil War – various Mujahideen factions (Afghan resistance fighters) fought against the USSR and its Soviet-backed Afghan ruler Babrak Karmal and later Dr. Najibullah.
- 1979 – Soviet forces invaded Afghanistan to prop up a pro-Soviet government.
- 1988-1989 – The Soviet forces withdrew. The Geneva Peace Accords are signed by Afghanistan, the Soviet Union, US and Pakistan.
- 1989-1992 – Afghan Civil War – Various Mujahideen groups were fighting President Mohammad Najibullah and his People's Democratic Party of Afghanistan which was left over after the Soviet withdrawl.
- 1992-1996 – Different factions fought for power; also known as the Second Afghan Civil War took place from April

28, 1992 until September 27, 1996. A new interim Afghan government was to replace the Republic of Afghanistan of President Mohammad Najibullah backed by the UN. However, the Mujahideen with the support of KGB and forces in the Afghan army sabotaged the UN Peace Plan and entered Kabul one day before the execution of the plan. The Taliban occupied Kabul on September 27, 1996 establishing the Islamic Emirate of Afghanistan.

- 1996-2001 – The Taliban take over Afghanistan – under their rule:
  - Girls' access to education after age 8 was outlawed
  - Women were forbidden to work
  - Women were forced to cover their entire bodies in public including their faces (burkas)
  - Women were forbidden from seeing a male doctor unless accompanied by a male family member
  - Women were forbidden to speak loudly in public
  - It was made illegal to display an image of a woman in public or within the home

> There were public beatings, amputations and executions
- 2001-2021 – War in Afghanistan – armed conflict launched in response to the September 11, 2001 attacks. US President Bush called for a marshall-like plan to reconstruct Afghanistan. After the Taliban were defeated in 2001, there was measurable improvement in Afghan women's rights and their position in society; establishment of a Ministry of Women's Affairs.
- 2002 – Schools reopened.
- 2011 Summer – Canadian troops withdrew from Afghanistan.
- 2020 – US and Taliban signed a peace agreement in Qatar that included withdrawal of US and NATO troops from Afghanistan, a Taliban pledge to prevent Al-Qaeda from operating in areas under Taliban control, and talks between the Taliban and Afghan government that began in September 2020.
- August 15, 2021 – The Taliban took the country for the second time and systematically removed women's rights including the right to gather. For

example, beauty salons were closed.
- August 30, 2021 – The last of the US troops withdrew from Afghanistan.
- August 15, 2021 - 2024 – There was systematic removal of women's rights by the Taliban including removing their right to gather outside of the home, closing women-owned businesses, and removing women from government positions. The Ministry of Women's Affairs was eliminated and was turned into the Ministry of Vice and Virtue. Schools were closed for girls and they were only allowed to be educated up to grade 6.[1] [2]

1950s to Early 1970s

The 1950s to early 1970s was a time when Afghanistan was open, when the government enlisted foreign advisors. Afghan women were given the right to vote, were able to attend college in urban areas, could have jobs outside the home, could run businesses, and some even ventured into politics. Kabul was a cosmopolitan city where women wore mini-skirts and stockings. The 1960s

---

[1] For a detailed timeline and chronology of key events in Afghanistan go to https:/www.bbc.com/news/world-south-asia-12023253
[2] Go to https://www.npr.org/2021/08/19/1028472005/afghanistan-conflict-timeline - helpful overview of key historic events in Afghanistan from The Soviet War to Taliban Recapture by Hannah Bloch.

and 1970s were Afghanistan's "glory days".

Mustafa fondly recalled:

"I remember the 60s and 70s and my wife wearing a skirt and stockings. Women were driving and participating in sports. Kabul University had students from Iraq, Iran and many different countries. Kabul U was a very fashionable place."

Afghan Civil War – 1978 to 1992

In 1973 King Zahir Shah was overthrown in a coup and starting in the late 1970s there was civil war. The civil war lasted from 1978 to 1992. During that time the various Mujahideen factions fought against each other, and Afghanistan was an unpredictable and unsafe place.

Who Were The Mujahideen And What Were They Fighting For?

The Afghan Mujahideen were Islamic resistance groups who fought against the Democratic Republic of Afghanistan and the Soviet Union during the Soviet-Afghan War and the First Afghan Civil War. The term "Mujahideen" is used by Muslims to refer to those who engage in struggle for the sake of Islam. This is commonly referred to as jihad. The Afghan Mujahideen were composed of numerous groups that differed across ideological and/or ethnic lines, but were united by pro-Islamic and anti-communist goals.

TRUTHS AND CONTRADICTIONS

The roots of the Afghan War lay in the overthrow of the moderate government led for President Mohammad Daud Khan in April 1978 by left-wing officers led by Nur Mohammad Taraki. After that, power was shared by two Marxist-Leninist groups who had little popular support.

> *"The new government forged close ties with the Soviet Union, launched ruthless purges of all domestic opposition, and began extensive land and social reforms that were bitterly resented by the devoutly Muslim and largely anti-communist population."* [3]

In 1978 when the Communist regime took power in Afghanistan, Farzanah painfully shared how her father, because he was an army officer loyal to the previous government, was put in jail for about a year. The leader, Nur Muhammad Taraki, was very cruel. He had many prisoners killed. Every night everyone became quiet when the soldiers came to the building where her father was staying. If someone coughed or made noise the soldiers would take them out and kill them. Her father was finally released from prison because he had an influential relative in government. Her <u>father turned</u> down the opportunity to return to

[3] https://www.britannica.com/topic/mujahideen-Afghani-rebels

the army. He said his health was poor. He stayed home and started a private business in Kabul. He focused his efforts on educating all his children. He was a feminist. He supported his daughters to be educated. His mission was that his youngest daughter would get her Master's Degree.

In Farzanah's words:

> "I was worried for one or two years that my father would not be at home. I was so dependent on my father. He emphasized to me, 'You are the one who your sisters will follow.' My uncle (my mother's brother) was very supportive while my father was in jail."

At that time Farzanah shared that although she was a clever child and had, to that point done very well at school, when her father was imprisoned, her grades dropped.

Asadi recalled:

> "Before the Soviet invasion, a violent change in the government brought fear and uncertainty, but many of us still hoped that things would get better. Sadly, when the Russians invaded, that hope disappeared. The whole nation stood up together to fight against the Soviet forces, whom we called the Russian invaders."

The Russians invaded in January 1979.

TRUTHS AND CONTRADICTIONS
Soviet Forces Invasion and Rule 1979-1989

Mirwais shared his story of the Russian invasion. Mirwais was in high school when they invaded. From time to time an alarm would go off at school and all classes were told to leave immediately and to seek shelter. He shared:

> "It was terrifying, hearing the alarm and running home to possible safety. Life was so uncertain. One day an alarm pierced the relative silence, and we were told to find safety. This day was different. I remember looking up at the sky and seeing many Soviet airplanes above the city and hearing the deafening whir of the engines. ...
>
> "One of my friends told me to run to a nearby mosque that had a basement. About six of us ran together and hid in the basement. The explosions were deafening as bombs hit and rocked the building above us. We wondered whether we would make it out alive. At one point we started to have difficulty breathing. There was much dust and clearly a lack of oxygen. I felt like a caged animal. We then noticed that the entrance to the basement had collapsed. We were trapped for about twenty minutes with our hearts racing and sweat starting to

pour down our faces. Suddenly, I had an idea. Perhaps we could burrow our way through the rubble. We all started to dig like dogs searching for a bone and in no time, we created a small hole and soon made it large enough for our young bodies to climb through. We were relieved and shocked when we reached the outside. The mosque that had been was shattered completely, and the eight to ten people in the building at the time of bombing had obviously been killed."

Asadi, another member of my strategic planning team, shared his experiences with the Russians.

"I remember the unfortunate day when I awoke and shortly after at school one of my classmates told me the President, along with his family, had been killed by the Russians. The Russians had taken over. I was about 10 years old. I felt angry. My friend and I decided to struggle against the Russian invasion by any means.

The Russians were conducting military operations throughout Kabul and the countryside (killing people and destroying villages). We were against the Russians. We lived in a small town on a highway where the Russian military Caravan was heading toward other parts with countless tanks, military vehicles and numerous jets in the sky. I wanted to go to Pakistan and launch a jihad against the invaders. However, my father cautioned me against it. He said 'Pakistan will misuse you. Learn and educate yourself and empower yourself to serve Afghanistan by peaceful means.' So, I stayed in Afghanistan. ...

"The Russians established several councils of minority ethnicities and a Ministry of Ethnic Groups with representatives from different tribes. This, I believe, divided the country.

"Once the Russian invasion began in my area, all the tribal elders came together and agreed that no one could take revenge on fellow villagers. Instead, the focus should be on the withdrawal of invaders from our home [country]. The elders banded together and understood that they had a big responsibility to take care of our land. Before this, there was a mechanism to compensate or take revenge for example, the killing of the killer or one of his close family members which was a usual practice in Afghan society."

Benesh described her experience:

"In 1978 when the Russians took over

Afghanistan, I was a student at Kabul University. It was peaceful in Kabul at that time. There was a lot of freedom for women. A year later [when the Russians invaded Kabul] there was fighting in the provinces. Roads were closed so we couldn't reach our homes by road. We mainly flew in military airplanes. That was a dangerous time. Many university students were imprisoned because they were against the Communist regime."

Marlize shared her experience:

"When the Russians first came to Afghanistan I was at university. The first year we had a lot of freedom. Later the situation became unstable when the Mujahideen [Afghan resistance fighters] started firing rockets against the Russians and the situation deteriorated."

Experiences From 1992 To 1996:
Different Factions Fighting For Power

Zahra recalled the frightful day when the Mujahideen entered and captured Kabul on April 28, 1992. She shared:

"It was a regular weekday, and just the day before their entrance, we were still in school. However, once they entered the city, Kabul changed completely. Men with long beards, dirty faces, and large weapons mounted on Toyota pickup trucks roamed the streets. Some of these vehicles even had anti-tank weapons installed, and they sped through the city non-stop, patrolling with reckless abandon. Both men and women lived in terror. The dress code changed drastically—men were no longer allowed to wear pants and shirts, and women were forbidden from going outside unless they were fully covered, including their faces.

"Within days, horrifying rumors spread that the Mujahideen were taking girls and even married young women by force. In one tragic incident, a young woman jumped from the fourth floor of her building to escape an Uzbek militant who tried to abduct and rape her.

"Kabul was divided among various groups. The Shia groups controlled the west of the city, a Tajik group controlled the north and central areas, an Uzbek group controlled some central parts and the east, and a Pashtun-led group controlled the south. Shortly after, these groups started fighting among themselves to capture more parts of the city.

"I think it was in May or June 1993 that

schools briefly reopened just to allow us to take the final exams for the academic year that had been disrupted. By that time, my school had been turned into a military base, like so many other schools across the city. I recall we were called to take our exams in the Ministry of Education building."

In 1993 Farzanah's family left Afghanistan and emigrated as refugees to Iran. Because Farzanah couldn't find a job in Iran her family left for Pakistan in 1999 and stayed till the end of May 2003. That's when Farzanah's family returned to Afghanistan.

In the rose garden one lunchtime Farzanah shared the story of what it was like in Kabul when the civil war started. She stated:

"I was 25, Kabul was a most insecure place. I recall being terrified as thousands of rockets daily rocked the city. All but the northern part of the city was destroyed. Our family left Kabul along with thousands of others and headed to Iran due to the internal war and fighting between different Mujahideen groups and warlords. It took fifteen days by bus for us to reach Iran. The journey was difficult. It was winter and so cold on the bus. Different Mujahideen groups stopped the bus from time to time along the way. I wrapped myself in a large blanket and tried to hide my youngest sister Zahra. I could sense the fear in my father although on the outside he appeared strong. He later shared that he was afraid for his daughters and his wife that we would be raped or kidnapped. Fortunately, neither of these terrible things befell us."

Taliban Takeover #1
1996-2001

Before living and working in Afghanistan I had heard about the Taliban and that they had outlawed schooling for girls in the country, but I didn't know a lot more about them. Who were they? How and why had they gained power and when? One day while waiting for a meeting to start, I had the opportunity to ask Farzaad some of these questions.

Who are the Taliban?

Farzaad answered, "The Taliban are religious scholars who largely ran Madrasahs; religious schools that taught boys from poor families to read and write."

How did the Taliban gain power initially?

Farzaad told me that Mula Mohammad Omar started the Taliban at the end of 1994-1995. He was supported by the central government in

Kandahar.

Farzaad also shared that at the end of 1994 and beginning of 1995, the Mujahideen co-commander of Kandahar married a boy. People came to Mula Mohammad and other religious scholars who had studied at Madrasahs in Pakistan as they were concerned about this co-commander's marriage to a boy. They were also concerned as young girls and boys were being taken from their homes by the Mujahideen.

Mula Mohammad Omar and his forces killed the Mujahideen co-commander as his behaviour was deemed not acceptable and they "cleaned up" and took over Kandahar.

The whole country collapsed within 6 months.

The people were fed up with Mujahideen because there was no justice; everyone was being killed; there was no rule of law.

The Taliban took over and ruled Afghanistan from 1996 to 2001. Under their rule:

- Women were forced to cover their entire bodies in public including their faces; to wear burkas
- Women were forbidden to work outside the home
- After the age of 8, girl's education was outlawed

TRUTHS AND CONTRADICTIONS

- Women were forbidden to speak loudly in public
- It was illegal to display the image of a woman in public or within the home
- The severing of hands or even execution were prescribed as punishment for petty crimes [4]
- Non-Islamic artistic relics were destroyed [5]

Events Leading Up to The Taliban Taking The Country The First Time

Before the Taliban took over the country in 1996 there was internal conflict and no formal government. From 1992 to 1996 were the worst years. The government collapsed and handed over the army to Massud who couldn't keep it. There was internal conflict in Kabul. The Mujahideen were firing rockets toward various parts of Kabul, targeting innocent people from other tribes, subjecting them to torture, and even killing them. They were looting homes. Tragically, Massud's men committed acts of sexual violence against girls and young women.

Asadi recalled:

---

[4] Go to https://www.britannica.com/topic/Taliban for an interesting article on the Taliban, their origins, their policies and how they came to power

[5] Check out https://www.thoughtco.com/history-of-the-bamiyan-buddhas-195108 for an article on the Bamiyan Buddhas

"There were checkpoints on the roads. People were coming to Kabul from different villages. They were being robbed, insulted and being asked for money by different groups of Mujahideen. Religious hatred and tribal divisions grew.

"This was the reason the Taliban initially arose in Kandahar. Then they took over Kabul and almost the entire country. Unfortunately, they were backward people with no clear agenda for making a prosperous and developed Afghanistan. The Taliban had their own interpretation of Islam that prevented some basic human rights, especially for women and girls. But there was security when they took over. There was no more killing or bloodshed in the streets."

I asked Mustafa what it was like when the Taliban took over Afghanistan the first time. He responded:

"That was a bad experience. We were already suffering because of the conflict. There was widespread fighting in the street. There were robberies. We heard gunshots on the street we were living on. Initially when the Taliban took power everyone was so happy because crime was gone. There were no gunshots. But very slowly people got oppressed by some of the things the Taliban were doing [for example] lashing women publicly, asking men why they weren't bearded, and why women weren't wearing hijab."

Shahmeer shared his experience when the Taliban took over Afghanistan the first time.

"I was in Pakistan when the Taliban took over Afghanistan the first time, but I went on summer vacation (for 3 months) to Afghanistan in 1997-1998. Travel was difficult. The roads were not paved from the Pakistan border to Kabul (seven to eight hours). I thought to myself, one day we will get a better government in Afghanistan, and we will be able to pave this road. I spent one night in Kabul before heading to my home province. At that time, it was relatively peaceful. I was not wearing a hat. The Taliban told me I should always cover my head. It was not easy to move around. Most activities were inside people's houses. People refrained from moving about."

Marlize shared her experience.

"I was working in a hospital in Mazar-i-Sharif. I was on duty. It was the evening. We had ordered food, having not eaten since the morning. We heard that the security was getting worse. Then someone said the Taliban had entered the city. We were trying to decide what to do as we were eating. We were so hungry having done surgery all day. Fortunately, my female colleagues and I had brought burkas to work with us.

"Then, one male doctor offered to drive me and another female doctor home. We headed out. Military people stopped the vehicle. I was so scared. They ordered the male doctor to take them out of the city. He tried to deter them by saying this is a very old car. It might run out of petrol. [They let Marlize and her female colleague out of the car.] Undeterred, five Taliban got into the vehicle and sat with the doors open. Finally, the car did run out of gas, and they let the doctor go home. He had to walk a long way back to reach his home.

"I ran toward my home and reached it in about ten minutes. I was crying and worried about my male colleague.

"Initially the Taliban shot at any person or animal in front of them. For three days no one could go out. They beat some people to death and made a mountain of dead bodies. They asked people to carry the dead bodies to a grave. Some people never found their relatives.

"I had a poor family staying in my home. One of the men from that family was beaten. He was Hazara. I was worried the Taliban might find us and beat us too. But we took care of the man.

"The Taliban asked all women to stay at home, not study, and not work. That said, I was allowed to work as a doctor. They gave us an identity card so we could go to hospital by ourselves without a man accompanying us. We had to wear a burka."

Parwais shared his experience of being in Kabul when the Taliban took the country the first time.

"I returned to Kabul for medical school in 1996. My two other brothers were students with me. Life was difficult.

"The Taliban closed the student hostels; education used to be free. We could stay in the physical buildings but there was no electricity or running water.

"I recall one evening when my brothers went to someone's house and had a delicious meal. They returned home and told me all about it. I was disappointed I was unable to join them. There was little to eat.

"Small amounts of cheap food were available at night. The guard (an old man hired to guard the building) would bring food. He would mix the food together and sell it to the students for a minimal amount. But spices, such as green chilis, were free. Now I cannot taste spicy things because I consumed so many green chilis. I lived on small amounts of food and bread I had gotten from my mom in the village and bits of food from the guard. The guard gave me hot water which I mixed with the bread from my mom. I am still in touch with the guard."

US And UK Invasion Of Afghanistan And The Defeat Of The Taliban[6]

Triggered by the September 11th attacks, on October 7, 2001, the US and the UK invaded, defeated the Taliban and took control of Afghanistan. At that time US President Bush called for a Marshall-like plan to reconstruct the country. There was great improvement in Afghan women's rights and their position in society. A government Ministry of Women's Affairs was established.

---

6 For a detailed description related to the Afghanistan War and how 9/11 led to a twenty-year war visit: https://www.iwmorg.uk/history/afghanistan-war-how-did-911-lead-to-a-20-year-war

In 2002, schools reopened. A number of women gained posts in government and had freedom of movement and rights they hadn't had under the Taliban.

This lasted until August 15, 2021, when the Taliban took the country for the second time.

Taliban Takeover #2

In 2021 the Taliban quickly began gaining power province by province until they arrived in Kabul and took over the Presidential palace on August 15, 2021. The world was shocked and surprised when the Taliban took over Afghanistan for the second time.

I asked some members of the strategic planning team what that experience was like for them.

Zahra stated:

> "It was a fearful, horrible experience. It got worse when I received emails and WhatsApp calls from people who wanted to help me get out of the country. They warned me to delete all emails and advised me to destroy my Fulbright certificate, but I didn't. I lived under a constant state of stress. It was chaotic; you never knew what would happen next. Some of my contacts were evacuated. I was alone in the family home and found it challenging to sleep. The few times I went out to buy

food I wore a long hijab and a mask.

"I was working at UNICEF and finally they arranged for me and a number of other single women to leave on a UN flight that flew from Kabul to Islamabad where UNICEF opened a satellite office."

Another colleague Mirwais shared his experience.

"On August 15 we came to the office like any other normal day. I was working for UNICEF at the time. I sent my son to a government office in the morning to verify a document. At around 10 am he called and told me that all the civil servants had left the building because the Taliban had entered the city. I shared this with my security focal point, and he did not believe what I said. He insisted that this was not the plan. The Taliban would instead come to the gates of Kabul, stay there for 2 months and then there would be a peaceful handover.

"Normally the UN would ask their staff members to stay home if there was a security threat. The security focal point denied that anything unusual was happening. Then Mirwais heard from another friend that the Taliban had entered the huge prison and were releasing all the prisoners. Finally, after calling several more people, the security focal point realized the Taliban were in fact in the city. He then advised UN staff to stay in the building that had bunkers.

"I told the security focal point that I had to go home to be with my family. I took my car and started driving. A route that usually took me 10 minutes took 4 hours. It was chaos in the streets, like an apocalypse. I was constantly calling my wife. When I reached home, we heard some bad things the Taliban had done.

"I told my kids to lock the door and not open it to anyone. The first night was horrible. I didn't know what was going to happen next. I saw Taliban with beards and long hair and weapons patrolling the streets. In the next few days, I received an email from the Canadian embassy to go to the airport and that there were military planes that would help me, and my family leave the country. I asked my son to check the airport. He checked the gate and said it was calm. We packed our belongings and called a taxi.

"When we arrived at the airport there were about 20,000 people to the left of the gate. I tried three times to enter the airport, and I couldn't. Then I found someone who said he could help me. He advised us to try the next day in the evening. We were then able to get through the crowd of people. We arrived at 1 am and stayed till the morning. At 8 am there were a group of Taliban who said there was a security threat, and we needed to go home. The next day we heard there was an explosion at the airport and many people were killed.

"Then I received an email from the Canadian embassy telling us to stay at home. I then got a Pakistani visa and tried to go to Pakistan. Still, we weren't able to leave the country."

Shahmeer described his experience of being in Kabul when the Taliban took the country in 2021.

"I was in Kabul. It was doomsday. Everything fell apart. People were running in the street. We had a small number of staff in our office. I told two women who worked with me to go home and regularly called them. I got a call from my wife. She said there was chaos in the streets. I told her I would walk home. Everyone was running and walking. I walked home.

"In the evening the Taliban appeared on our road and came to the front of our apartment. They were coming to take the armoured vehicles. We had a two-storey basement in our building, and we had 30 or 40 armoured vehicles parked there, that belonged to government officials. The Taliban took these vehicles by force. It was scary. I was afraid of losing my life. I had nightmares that I would die, and my twin daughters would be fatherless. I was also worried about friends who worked in the government. Social activism was coming back. I was worried that the Taliban would come after me about things I had written online in the past opposing them."

Farzaad had an incredible story to tell. When asked what his experience was like he shared:

"It was harsh. My beard became white in three months (from October to December 2021) from the collapse till I came out of Afghanistan. We were not expecting this to happen so quickly. We were looking for an agreement to happen without violence and were supporting the peace talks.

"For a few weeks I was not in my home.

I was in the office. We had a meeting with the Minister. We spoke and the Minister gave us a task to make a new MOU to sign with a foreign ambassador to send scholars to his country to study. Suddenly around 1 pm, the head of office security said the Taliban were coming in the front door. We left through the back door. We walked for 30 minutes until my brother came with his car. Then I left my home and went to my sister's (new) house. I stayed there for about one and a half weeks. Only my brother and mother knew where I was. Even my wife did not know where I was. Then I returned to my home and lived only on the third floor. I was working with the EU and others to get out of the country. And then we were taken to Mazar to leave. The Taliban grabbed me out of a plane. Then we returned to Kabul. When I was going to meet an agent to get a Pakistan visa and was in my brother's car, the Taliban caught me again.

"The Taliban were taking people from their homes at night. No one knew where they were. Then a dead body would appear.

"We have 150 houses in my village.

Around sixty percent were supportive of the Taliban. Some community members didn't want us to live because they lost family members during the war, and because we had worked with the government, they thought we had caused the deaths of their family members."

I kept in touch with Mustafa over the years and typically sent him New Year's and Eid cards.[7] Occasionally I would send short emails. After the Taliban took Afghanistan in 2021, I wrote him and asked whether he and his family were planning to leave the country. He said he had investigated the possibility and found out that he did not have the financial resources to do so. My heart went out to him. I asked about his 23-year-old daughter who had an undergraduate degree. He responded that she stayed at home all day doing nothing; she was deeply depressed. I enquired whether she wrote as writing is therapeutic, but he answered no. I asked about his wife who he said was extremely religious and prayed 5 times a day. This woman who had gone to university in the "glory days" (the 1970s) and had worn skirts and stockings.

I asked where and how women could gather

---

[7] Eid in Arabic means feast or festival. There are two major eids in a calendar year celebrated in Muslim countries. To learn more visit: https://timesofindia.indiatimes.com/world/middle-east/explained-what-is-eid-and-how-do-muslims-celebrate-it/articleshow/82543512.cms

and he responded, only at the homes of relatives. I felt helpless. I wished there was some way I could help this special man and his family.

Since the takeover of the Taliban, they have systematically removed women's rights including removing their right to gather outside of the home, closing women-owned businesses and removing them from government positions, eliminating the Ministry of Women's Affairs and turning it into the Ministry for the Propagation of Virtue and the Prevention of Vice, and closing schools for girls and only allowing them to be educated up to grade 6.

When the Taliban took the country in 2021, many Afghans who I had worked with or knew in the Ministry got in touch and asked me how they could get out of the country. I sent them the information I had. Many of them wanted to immigrate to Canada but this was only possible if they had worked for a Canadian entity such as the Canadian Embassy or the Canadian military. I wrote a number of letters of recommendation. Some of my strategic planning team were fortunate to be accepted and immigrated as refugees to Canada. I was able to raise money through friends and family to support another colleague to immigrate to Canada with his extended family (twenty-three in all). My heart goes out to the many Afghan women and men who want to leave

Afghanistan but are trapped there.

Chapter 13
MISSION #2

My strategic planning team tried to get me to return to Afghanistan for several years after my departure. I conceded to virtually backstopping[8] the team for about six months. Unfortunately, the internet was not great during that time. It seemed like every five minutes the connection would be broken. It was frustrating! I did a lot of emailing back and forth with my team in an attempt to continue building their capacity.

I never thought I would return to Kabul, but one of my colleagues who knew of my work got in touch. She and her organization had received a grant, and she needed someone with on the ground experience in the health sector in Afghanistan to be on the team. After some cajoling, I realized that she was desperate, so I conceded. Our "team" for this mission consisted of myself and a thirty-something man named James with a newly "minted" doctorate. He had experience in conflict zones and had an open and engaging personality.

---

8 Backstopping is the process of providing technical and managerial support to a project.

Before departing we had several conference calls.

Much of our task was to interview key officials in the Ministry and other related agencies and formulate recommendations based on those interviews. Many of them I knew and had previously worked with. It made sense that I would take the lead in the interviews already having a relationship with the people. I asked James when he interviewed if he typically hand-wrote the responses or typed them on a laptop at the same time. He responded that he typically hand-wrote and transcribed later. I said, "If you do that, every evening we will have to spend about three hours transcribing the day's interviews." He reflected and said, "I can and will type on the laptop while you take the lead interviewing." This approach worked extremely well. Each evening we would review his notes from the day, add our perceptions, and plan for the following day. We got a lot of valuable information and turned out to be a great team.

I remember clearly the experience of entering the compound, the place we would be sleeping and eating during our stay. I was surprised to see not only one, but two high walls and metal gates surrounding the compound. In addition to checking for bombs under our vehicle with long mirrors, the guards had huge black sniffer dogs.

After getting through the second gate, I noted a number of UN vehicles lined up in the parking lot. They were white Toyota Land Cruisers with UN in large blue letters etched across their sides. I immediately felt ill at ease as UN vehicles are often targeted and blown up.

On my return to Kabul in 2015, many of the people I had worked with had been promoted. Mustafa was now a Deputy Minister, and more women were in Director's posts. Farzanah was head of a department. My heart was full when she revealed that she had used the strategic planning process she had learned from me to develop the strategic plan for her department. It had worked so well that she didn't need to hire any outside consultants, except for one to translate the strategy from Dari to English.

I could sense on my first day back at the Ministry that many people I connected with felt happy to see me. I certainly was delighted to see them. I sensed one man wanting to reach out and hug me (definitely not an action that is taken in Muslim countries). He reached out and squeezed my hand so tightly. This, in a culture where some Muslim men refuse to shake women's hands for fear of being tempted by them. That happened to me once in Pakistan when one of the well-educated Pakistani consultants whose wife had a

PhD refused to shake my hand when I offered it and said, "I don't shake women's hands." That was rather brutal. It made me cautious in future to reach out and offer a strong handshake to Muslim men.

Chapter 14
TRUTHS AND CONTRADICTIONS

Based on the interviews with Afghan colleagues, my own experiences in the country, and doing some online research, a number of contradictions emerged I feel called to share. This section highlights these findings. I invite you to decide what is a truth and what is a contradiction.

Tribalism is divisive and negatively impacts the lives of Afghan men and women.

Afghanistan consists of a number of ethnolinguistic groups. The four main tribes are Pashtu, Tajik, Hazara and Uzbek.

Many of the writings about Afghanistan state that Afghanistan is a tribal country and internal struggles among the various tribes prevent the formation of a stable state. For example, in Angelo Rasanayagam's *Afghanistan – A Modern History* (2003), He cites the words of Sir Henry Rawlinson, a British general:

"The nation consists of a mere collection of tribes, of unequal power and divergent habits, which are held together, more or less loosely, according to the personal character of the chief who rules them. The feeling of patriotism, as known in Europe, cannot exist among Afghans, for there is no common country."[9]

I asked many of my Afghan colleagues which tribe they belong to and how that has shaped or influenced them and their life experiences. All of them stated that the tribe they were born into did not influence how they related to people from other tribes.

Here are some typical responses:

"I was born Pashtu, but my father never differentiated us (from others). We were taught and learned to get along and value everyone."

"I'm Pashtu, yet I have friends who are from different tribes, and they are all my friends who I value and admire."

"I was raised in Kabul with many ethnic

---

9 Rasanayagam, Angelo. Afghanistan- A Modern History, New York: I.B. Tauris, 2003, xvi-xvii.

groups and have friends from all different ethnic groups. I think it is a waste of time thinking about these things. The negative view of tribalism started when the British were ruling and had influence inside Afghanistan. Many feel the British had a policy of divide and rule and many Afghans think this is so."

Another said: "After the Russian invasion there was a plan to divide people and rule; to poison one tribe against another."

"I am Pashtu, and we speak Dari at home. My second mom is Tajik. She is a Persian. There are myths that these tribes are divided. This is not so. Afghans live together and have lived for centuries beside each other. The politicians make things bigger. If you go to the local level, you will not see these divisions."

"My father was Pashtu and my mother Tajik. We spoke Dari. We lived in harmony. No one ever cared about their tribe."

"I am Tajik. I love to speak Pashtu when I see a friend who is speaking Pashtu. When I enter a group because I am Tajik, they all speak Dari. I usually work at the community level. I have never felt that people don't want to speak Dari. This [tribalism] is used as an instrument to divide people."

"My father was Pashtu, and my mother was Arab. She was very beautiful. My father was an open-minded person. That's why he chose a woman from another tribe. My mother was religious. She was from a religious family and was literate. When we were at school my father told my mother to become a teacher, but my mother was shy and preferred to stay at home. My mother was very strict and always controlled us."

"My father said Hazara's are smart and honest people. Their kids are hardworking, and we need to learn from them. My Dad's closest friends were from different tribes. …In general, Afghan people love and have strong connections with others from different tribes. Tribalism is not an issue for them."

According to Farzaad:

"There were no issues [with tribalism] before the Russians withdrew. It happened during the civil war. Tribalism has increased in the past 20 years. After 2001 when the Taliban were defeated, the politicians started to give more fuel to tribalism. The Taliban are only bound by a religious ideology. The others are using ethnicity to divide."

Zahra reflected about how life was for Afghans before 1991:

> "... before the Mujahideen took control and began their house-to-house fighting for power in Kabul. I was a teenager at the time. Schools closed for a year due to the intense fighting, but when they reopened, something had profoundly changed. When my classmates and I reunited, we began to see each other and our teachers based on tribal belonging and whether we were Sunni or Shia. I was shocked because just a year earlier, none of us cared about these things. Tribal affiliation or sectarian differences had never been part of our conversations or even our consciousness. This deep division was introduced to us by the Mujahideen. I believe Western countries supporting them, particularly the US and Iran, played a significant role in fostering these divisions through their financial support to Mujahideen."

The Quran states that women are not to be educated, and Muslim men are not supportive of their daughters being educated.

Based on how the Taliban are currently governing Afghanistan you would think that women are meant to be kept at home, controlled, and not educated according to the Quran.

All the Afghan colleagues I spoke with, both men and women, did not share that belief or have that experience growing up. Here are some of their comments.

Zahra emphasized:

"There are certain cultural practices that dominate Islam that are not currently happening in Afghanistan. For example, "Islam says education and literacy is for everyone."

Amina shared:

"Islam encourages men and women to go to school. Our prophet Mohammad's wife was a businesswoman."

Sandra Gathmann, a US journalist, interviewed women and government officials in December 2022 more than a year after the Taliban had taken control of Afghanistan.[10] In her documentary she asked

---

10 Check out https://www.youtube.com/watch?v=o95Mt48x-VgM&t=65s – What Women in Afghanistan want you to know – Aljazeera English

the Head of the Ministry of Vice and Virtues, previously the Ministry of Women's Affairs, why women had been removed from their government positions and why the Ministry of Women's Affairs closed down given that Mohammad's wife was a businesswoman and the Quran supports the education of women and men. He responded, "We believe in Islam and Islam has given women the permission for education … and also the permission to work. Restrictions on girls' education and women's work is only temporary – not official policy. For example, we're working out how to separate men and women in government offices."

Farzanah revealed to me that the Quran does not state that men have control over women but rather that men and women are equal.

> "My father focussed his efforts on educating all his children. He was a feminist and supported all his daughters to be educated. Today we all are doctors and several of us have Master's degrees. … [When I was young] I travelled with my father. He showed us that we could speak with men and present ourselves in society and community. He always encouraged us to take the lead at special events."

Zahra contributed:

"Education was key in our home. My father was always giving us rewards and appreciation. The first gift my father gave me was a notebook and pencil."

Amina shared:

"In my context nine out of ten families keep their wife as a queen. I was a princess to my dad. I never felt that as a woman I could not do what a man can do."

Marlize stated:

"My mother and father were well educated, and education was so important in my family. My siblings and I were always top of our class in school."

Zahra shared:

"Islam says education and literacy is for everyone. … Islam gives rights to women including inheriting land from parents; this is not happening in Afghanistan."

She also shared:

"What is going on right now is unfortunately the ideology of many Afghans. Before I left Afghanistan in 2021, I travelled to seventeen provinces and what is now formal was what was imposed rurally on girls by their families before the Taliban took power in 2021."

In Benesh's words,

"The Islam the Taliban is imposing is not written in the Quran."

Amina shared:

"Everything the Taliban are doing is against Islam; restricting women from their normal life. This is highly impacting the maternal mortality rate in the country, e.g. restricting women from seeking health care….

"Before the Taliban took over, they killed people. It is prohibited to kill a human being in Islam. Islam is all about happiness and kindness. It is against killing people."

According to Farzaad:

"Before 1979 we had kingdoms; they were Islamic. We had universities, women were working in government and in the private sector; they were doing sports abroad. People were living peacefully together. After 1997 the meaning of religion changed. The Saudis brought their type of Islam to Afghanistan which is a very strict version of shariah law."

Illiterate Muslim women cannot be strong leaders/influencers.

Mirwais shared:

> "My mom was illiterate, yet she was a strong advocate for education. All her sons went to university and all my sisters finished high school. … During the civil war people struggled and food was scarce. My Mom [during that time] thought about saving money for [our] education. My mom was a true leader. She negotiated conflicts within the family from a young age. She was well respected by all the villagers."

Asadi revealed:

> "My grandmother who was illiterate supported poor people. She expressed love and was deeply concerned about humanity and especially marginalized people."

Zahra shared the story of how the mother of a friend fought with the males in her family to ensure girls got educated above grade 6. After her husband died this woman gave her daughter money to go to university.

TRUTHS AND CONTRADICTIONS

Afghans are very harsh people and are not peaceful by nature.

According to Mirwais:

"Afghans are not harsh, and they are not extremists. ... My father is a moderate Muslim and religious person. I never heard from him that someone should be harmed based on their religious belief. ... Before the Soviet invasion, Afghans were not like the Taliban and Mujahideen. ... Afghans try their best to contribute to overall development in the world. We seek education and to serve humanity."

Asadi shared:

"Almost all Afghans are Muslims. They have a traditional understanding of Islam. ... When I was a child, kindness, supporting each other, charity and tolerance were taught and believed in. ... After the Russian invasion, some of the sentiments of jihad and fighting against invaders were strengthened. They resisted against British, Russians, and Americans due to Islam. Before this these people were moderate Muslims. They believed if you do good things you will go to Paradise and if you insult or rob others, God will not forgive you and you will go to hell."

In Farzaad's words:

"In Afghanistan we have an Afghan Code of Conduct. When there was no government, we governed ourselves according to this code, which is similar to Islamic rules. [For example], if you kill someone you will be killed or [would need to] get a pardon from the family. If you attack someone's house, you must pay back [the damage] you did. … There is a saying we have that if you are not honest to your God you will not be honest to anyone. Most people pray five times a day. We do have people who don't pray five times a day and, in the past, they were not forced to do so. What the Taliban is doing is forcing people to pray five times a day. Forcing men to have a beard. The Taliban are interfering in our personal lives in ways that are against Afghan culture. For example, we have a national dance and our own instruments. The Taliban are now banning our traditional music."

Mirwais shared:

"All Afghans aspire to live a good life. During the republic (2001-2021), we thought Afghanistan was moving toward a path of prosperity and development."

According to Marlize: "Half of the Quran is taken from other religions and other prophets. … It states that Muslims should be kind, honest and respect others."

Under the current Taliban rule there is no education for girls past Grade 6 and professional women are unable to practice other than those who teach girls up to Grade 6 in elementary school.

Marlize shared that she made three trips to Afghanistan for family events including a wedding and a funeral in 2023. She dressed in black from head to toe and had no trouble travelling from Kabul to her home village. She covered when she went out and didn't go out much. She shared a number of her learnings from those visits including:

"The International Rescue Committee (IRC) supported the training of health technicians through the Institute of Health Sciences for two years after the Taliban takeover. However, they have stopped their funding. Now, there are private institutions that teach women and men dentists, nurses, technologists, and midwives in a 2-year program that the Taliban allows. …

"In the first year the Taliban were in power (i.e. from August 2021 to August 2022), they did not close the university in our province. They closed it in the second year. They closed the universities in Kabul in the first year."

Marlize's cousin who is an obstetrician/gynecologist is still allowed to practice in the women's section of her hospital.

Marlize shared that:

"The Taliban are slowly cutting the salaries of women schoolteachers and university lecturers. That said, most women teachers even if they are not teaching are currently receiving a meager salary [e.g. $73 US per month].

"Women are currently in prison in their homes. Illiterate women have zero opportunity."

Wearing hijab (a covering worn by some Muslim women to cover their hair) is a required practice of Islam.

Wearing covered clothing such as the hijab, niqab, or burka, is not a required Isalmic convention. Men and women are expected to dress modestly, however veiling is not considered one of the five pillars of Islam. There is debate on the extent of a woman's covering and proper attire— does it include the entire body? The entire head and face? Therefore a hijab is not necessarily required as it depends on the interpretations of the Islamic law as well as the geographic location, the civil laws, and personal choice.

Afghans have demonstrated they can govern themselves and live in harmony. Outside invaders have created the conflict and divisions within the country.

Afghanistan is a rich country with many natural resources. It is centrally located and due to its geographic location has encouraged invaders, and Afghans to fight against and resist these invaders.

As one of my strategic planning team stated:

> "The uniqueness of our people is that they can regulate their lives. This was demonstrated in the past 45 years and in the 19th century. People followed their traditional rules and systems and lived in harmony treating each other with respect and keeping their own lands and boundaries. This was due to Islam and Pashtun Wali [an unwritten Pashtu code] … Once the Russian invasion began, in my area all the tribal elders came together and agreed that no one should take

revenge. The people banded together and acknowledged the big responsibility they had to take care of the land."

Another said:

"Afghanistan is a crossroad to empires. Conquer Afghanistan first and then move to conquer another country. … Afghanistan has been in war and conflict for most of its' life."

Another colleague shared:

"In 1992 when the government collapsed, slowly the warlords became dominant; they misused people and motivated them by tribalism. They looted and collected resources for themselves. … There were groups of Mujahideen in the villages. Since there was no government, the warlords could use their power. They were independent and irresponsible people."

Still another stated:

"We had a peace council for 20 years, but they didn't succeed to bring peace to the country. Corruption spoiled the system from the inside out. It was unfortunate. We lost a tremendous opportunity for progress and development."

TRUTHS AND CONTRADICTIONS
The current situation in Afghanistan is dire.

According to Marlize:
"The Taliban has 70,000 members and they occupy a country of 40 million people. People become so desperate because no one is hearing their voice; there is no freedom of speech. People have become so poor. They are struggling for food. If you keep them poor, they don't have the strength to speak out. … it is so painful. If 10 million people die in Afghanistan nobody cares. You don't see any future. I became a refugee for five years and suffered a lot. I live in pain. I will leave this world with this pain.

"I left Afghanistan in 2012 to study public policy and the philosophy of politics. My dream was to return as a female politician. But my dream broke because the country situation became worse and worse. My family said don't come, your life may be at risk. Three days before we were scheduled to return to Afghanistan, we cancelled our tickets realizing that the risk was too great."

In Mustafa's words:

"NGO's [non-governmental organizations] in general are facing huge problems. Work is challenging and projects are of short duration. [The Taliban] make you sign MOUs [Memorandums of Understanding]. Our NGO continues to work in 13 provinces. In one province they have asked women not to come to the office, they should work from home. Sometimes they want us to accept people they introduce. …

"Afghanistan has very high illiteracy. For that reason, everyone accepts what our religious leaders and scholars say. Almost 99 percent of the country are Muslim. The other one percent are Hindus and Sikhs. Many people are strong believers but don't have religious education or knowledge of religious issues. They have blind faith. …

"People are financially unable to leave Afghanistan. We don't have an idea of the percentage of people who wish to leave the country. …

"I lost hope the first time when Afghanistan was taken by the Taliban. Everything can change any time. We thought it would take months for the

Taliban to take over (in 2021) and they did it in one day. We lose (are losing) so many daughters. What will happen to women and girls in Afghanistan?"

Amina shared that her parents and some of her siblings are still in Afghanistan:

"Security wise, things are better than before. Everyday three or four bomb attacks were happening before. But poverty is increasing; there are almost zero job opportunities. Women are not allowed to work, they stay home. There are also fewer jobs available for men. They largely survive by selling vegetables or starting small businesses. … Girls' education is a huge concern."

Benesh contributed:

"I am worried about Afghan children. The education is focusing on religious studies leading to brainwashing especially in the rural areas. … The Taliban are receiving support from the outside. … Our country is being forgotten. It is a political issue."

According to an email from the Georgetown Institute for Women Peace and Security from August 15, 2021 to August 15, 2024, "Taliban authorities have enacted approximately 100 edicts and orders that virtually confine women to their homes and prevent them from accessing education, employment, or participation in public life. Under these restrictions, Afghan women and girls face deteriorating mental and physical health, increasing domestic violence, and the pervasive threat of violence and arrest for allegedly violating edicts." [11]

---

[11] https://www.usip.org/tracking-talibans-Mistreatment-women

Chapter 15

PERSONAL REFLECTIONS

Having not been in Afghanistan since 2015, I still vividly feel the emotions related to certain events I experienced, and from the stories shared with me by my Afghan colleagues. I also have much respect for the courage and resilience of the Afghans I have worked with.

I feel pain and sadness for the following:

- For all those women young and old in Afghanistan who can no longer gather or speak publicly; for those who can no longer work after having satisfying careers; for those who were just starting their careers when the Taliban took the country on August 15, 2021, and now can only sit at home and do domestic duties

- For those women who feel so depressed, who have lost hope for a future like the recent past when women had high level and fulfilling careers, could own their own businesses, could move about relatively freely, and could share their own views

and perspectives
- For the men who feel helpless and yet see no way out
- For the young girls who can only go to school to grade 6, many of whom will be forced into early marriages and never be able to find their passions and share their unique gifts with the world
- For the many illiterate women who live in rural Afghanistan who blindly follow what the Taliban tell them to do in the name of Islam and must wear a burka
- For those women who want a better life for themselves and their daughters
- For the men who have daughters, are unable to leave Afghanistan and wish there was something more they could do
- For those men and women who although they have worked for a Canadian, US, or UK entity do not have the funds to leave Afghanistan and get themselves and their families to another country, or the financial resources to support themselves and their families while they are waiting to start new lives in Canada, the US and other western nations
- For those women and men who were able to leave Afghanistan and start new lives

but do not have the resources to bring family members to join them

- For those who when they come to Canada or the US, long to return to their homeland. Sometimes it is a husband who wants to return, and the wife and daughters who want to stay; for those families who are torn apart
- For those Afghan women and men who have come to Canada as refugees and are unable to use their years of experience as doctors, nurses, etc. without studying again and getting new credentials
- For those women and men who have had their assets frozen since leaving Afghanistan
- For those applying again and again for positions they are more than qualified for and who keep getting letters of rejection
- For the many Afghan refugees who have no hope for the future of their country.

Chapter 16

THE FUTURE OF AFGHANISTAN: THE WAY FORWARD

Given the current state of Afghanistan, what is the future of Afghanistan?

Speaking with my Afghan colleagues, the majority feel there is no hope for Afghanistan. The country they grew up in and love is doomed.

One man shared:

> "Afghanistan has always been under attack due to its' geopolitical position – in the middle of Asia that connects one part of Asia to other parts, and [because] it has many resources. Due to this, Afghanistan may never face peace and security. Because many of our people are illiterate. Our neighbours want to keep us like this. The people in power do not want the country to move forward. History keeps repeating itself."

Another voiced that he can't be sure. He shared:

> "I lost hope when Afghanistan was taken by the Taliban the first time. Everything can change at any time. We thought it would take months for the Taliban to take over and they did it (the second time) in one day."

What can we learn from the past and what has happened in Afghanistan and in other conflict-ridden countries to help us move toward a more peaceful, humanitarian world free of war and open conflict?

According to Nabi Sahak, in his article *The Talibanisation of Afghanistan: A Repeat of History in the Making:*

> "… Afghanistan's neighbours … would do well to draw lessons from history and adopt a genuine policy of cooperation and development in Afghanistan – one that sees the country as a regional hub for connectivity and trade, not as a battlefield of conflicting political interests. Supporting Afghanistan in such a positive direction is not only the right thing to do, but it would also ensure that the war-torn country finally has a chance

TRUTHS AND CONTRADICTIONS

to live in peace and, most importantly, to become a partner in regional growth and stability."[12]

What can the international community do?

- Support the United Nations Refugee Agency (UNHCR) and Richard Bennett's work (Special Rapporteur on the situation of human rights in Afghanistan) who has "... urged the international community to stand together for the human rights of the people of Afghanistan."[13]
- Induce the Taliban to end gender apartheid in Afghanistan.[14]
- Urge member states to support increased international aid to Afghanistan.
- Designate gender apartheid as a crime against humanity and codify it into law.

---

12 https://rusi.org/explore-our-research/publications/commentary/talibanisation-afghanistan-repeat-history-making

13 Afghanisan: UN expert calls on international community to prioritise human rights of Afhans in any 'normalisation' OHCHR

14 Gender apartheid refers to the systemic oppression, discrimination, and segregation of a specific group based on gender." - https://www.cfr.org/in-brief/how-talibans-rule-fueling-movement-end-gender-apartheid

What can you do?

You can donate to organizations such as:

- **Right to Learn Afghanistan** – https://righttolearn.ca/ – founded in 1996 and previously called Canadian Women for Women in Afghanistan offers virtual courses for women and girls and aims to make the right to education a reality for Afghan girls and women.
- **Georgetown Institute for Women Peace and Security** – https://giwps.georgetown.edu/ – is a centre for research and advocacy that focuses on women's role in building peace and preventing conflict. It regularly produces the Women Peace and Security Index that scores and ranks women's security, inclusion and justice in 177 countries around the globe.
- **Women for Women International** – https://www.womenforwomen.org – This global community empowers women who have endured war and conflict by equipping them with the social and economic skills needed to rebuild their lives. These women share their knowledge with others, fostering a more equitable world where every woman's voice is heard, her role recognized, and her contributions

respected.

- **UN Women** – https://www.unwomen.org/en/about-us – UN Women is a United Nations organization focused on promoting gender equality and empowering women. As a global advocate for women and girls, it was created to fast-track efforts in addressing their needs.

- **UN Refugee Agency (UNHCR)** – https://www.unhcr.org/ – A global organization committed to saving lives, defending rights, and creating a better future for individuals forced to leave their homes due to conflict and persecution. They spearhead international efforts to safeguard refugees, displaced communities, and stateless individuals.

- **Women for Afghan Women** – https://womenforafghanwomen.org/afghanistan/ – In collaboration with strategic partners and local stakeholders, Women for Afghan Women (WAW) delivers humanitarian aid, mental health care, protection, and support services to vulnerable groups throughout Afghanistan. Their efforts primarily focus on women, internally displaced individuals, returning refugees, and their children and families.

What More Can You Do?

- You can volunteer with local chapters that organize fundraising and awareness-raising events such as: the Red Pashmina Walk of Right to Learn Afghanistan – https://righttolearn.ca/
- Host fundraisers or awareness-raising events in your neighborhood, e.g. for Women for Afghan Women - https://womenforafghanwomen.org/afghanistan/
- Volunteer as an intern with organizations supporting women and girls in Afghanistan
- Volunteer as a Board member with organizations supporting Afghan women and girls
- Take part in one of UN Women's campaigns https://www.unwomen.org/en/about-us
- Raise awareness on social media
- You can sponsor Afghan families as refugees to resettle in Canada, US, or the UK (Check with the appropriate government agency in your country about how to do this).
- You can support Afghan women, girls and their families when they resettle in your country by providing them with furniture, bedding, clothing, etc., and connecting with them regularly to support them

emotionally as well as physically with their resettlement.

- You can connect with immigrant aid agencies in your area to identify women and families who are recent arrivals and could benefit from support.

My Vision

Here is my vision that I hope you connect with and share with others to build connections based on our common humanity.

> I see a world free of war and violence.
>
> One where all cultures and religions are accepted.
>
> Where all people are respected and treated with respect.
>
> Where people live together in communities that model the values of contribution, collaboration, caring and connection.
>
> Where people are truly connected with who they are and the gifts they have to share.
>
> Where creativity is valued, and everyone knows how to tap into and express their creative side.
>
> Where people have the courage to reach

out for support when they need it.

I see a world where people trust their bodies, value their own wisdom, and know how to say no.

One that believes in the power of groups and synergy.

That the whole is greater than the sum of the parts.

A world where women and men stand together as partners.

I believe each one of us has a role to play, whether it be big or small, to move toward a world of peace and understanding.

What will you do to help build peace in the world and improve the lot of women and girls in Afghanistan?

Also by Pamela Thompson

Learning to Dance with Life: A Guide For High Achieveing Women includes seven keys and proven tools and practices to support women to transform their lives from constantly "doing" and "giving" to healthy, balanced lives THEY design and love. It emerged from the author's own experience of burning out, and includes intimate stories from her personal life, and tools she has used herself and with clients around the world, as a coach and consultant.

The Exploits of Minerva part memoir, part personal growth guide, explores through raw, real, life-altering and empowering stories, six women in a Women's Circle who have supported one another for over two decades through various life transitions.

About The Author

Pamela Thompson B.N. (McGill), M.Sc. (University of Edinburgh) is a seasoned global health and management consultant, author and visionary leader who has lived and worked on five continents, including in conflict zones. Driven by a lifelong curiosity about people, cultures, and countries, she has dedicated her career to fostering positive change in complex environments. From co-creating national strategies to managing large international development projects, Pamela has collaborated with governments, NGOs, and international organizations like the World Health Organization and the Ministry of Public Health in Afghanistan.

Pamela is founder of Female Wave of Change Canada – https://fwoccanada.com, a national non-profit dedicated to building a more equitable and sustainable world through the power of feminine leadership. She is also the creator of the "Art of Change Framework," a transformative process that supports mission-driven women to navigate life's crossroads with clarity and confidence.

Pamela is the author of two bestselling books "Learning to Dance with Life: A Guide for High Achieving Women" and "The Exploits of Minerva: Reflections of a Sixty-Something Woman".

When she's not writing, Pamela enjoys being in nature, travelling and inspiring audiences through experiential workshops, podcast guest appearances, and speaking engagements. For more insights and resources and to access her "Art of Change Framework", visit https://pamela-thompson.com.

www.ingramcontent.com/pod-product-compliance
Lightning Source LLC
LaVergne TN
LVHW011709060526
838200LV00051B/2822